THE COMPLETE
SOURDOUGH COOKBOOK

Also by DON HOLM

Old-Fashioned Dutch Oven Cookbook

Pacific North!

101 Best Fishing Trips in Oregon

The COMPLETE SOURDOUGH COOKBOOK

for camp, trail, and kitchen

by

DON AND MYRTLE HOLM

Authentic and Original Sourdough Recipes
from the Old West

The CAXTON PRINTERS, Ltd.
CALDWELL, IDAHO
1976

First printing July, 1972
Second printing April, 1973
Third printing May, 1974
Fourth printing June, 1975
Fifth printing October, 1976

Library of Congress Card No. 77-150816

International Standard Book Number 0-87004-223-8

Lithographed and bound in the United States of America by
The CAXTON PRINTERS, Ltd.
Caldwell, Idaho 83605
129071

I long for a whiff of bacon and beans, a snug
  shakedown in the snow;
A trail to break, and a life at stake, and
  another bout with the foe.

—Robert W. Service
"The Heart of the Sourdough"

FOREWORD

ONE ANOMALY of the Space Age and sophisticated microbiology is unprecedented renewed public interest in one of the oldest arts known to man—the use of a homemade yeast "factory" as the basis for all manner of wholesome, healthful, and delicious baked, fried and roasted foods.

This art is called "sourdough cooking," and it has been with us for somewhere between 4,000 and 6,000 years.

That is, up until about half a century ago when commercial yeast cakes became available for home use. With that the art of sourdough cooking began to fade away and, along with it, the quality of home baking.

For years sourdough baking was kept alive only on the frontier, on the farms and cattle ranches of the West, and in the logging and mining camps of Alaska and the Pacific Northwest. Elsewhere it was forgotten, as packaged bread and frozen TV dinners were substituted for the real, tasty, old-fashioned, wholesome ways and the word "sourdough" came to be known through Grade B movies and "Western" stories as a sobriquet for characters like those played by Gabby Hayes or Walter Brennan, complete with burro and pickax. In Alaska it came to mean a settler or prospector who had spit in the Yukon, killed a b'ar, and married a squaw.

Within the past decade, however, there has been an astonishing revival of interest in this old art. Maybe it is simply a reaction to the tasteless products of transistorized, homogenized modern urban society; maybe it is merely a nostalgic human longing for the good old days when life was simpler, values more basic, and food more wholesome.

The authors of this cookbook grew up on sourdough cookery. Through the years they have collected and preserved these authentic old recipes, few of which have ever been in print before, having been handed down for generations by word of mouth and custom. All have been thoroughly proven by years of use under original conditions; all have been tested and adapted where needed to modern kitchen use.

The first complete and original sourdough book of its kind, this volume tells everything folks nowadays want to know about this ancient and honorable cookery.

It certainly will help the user to discover a more wholesome, more tasty, and more satisfying world of home cooking.

And the key to it is a simple lactic acid micro-organism created in a crock of home-grown sourdough "starter," in some mysterious way—like life itself.

ACKNOWLEDGMENTS

The authors are most grateful to Edwin and Nadeen Whiteman of Oregon City, and Pearl and Reuben Gischler of Eugene for the many genuine Oregon Trail antiques used as props in photos.

CONTENTS

ILLUSTRATIONS

INTRODUCTION

As THIS WAS being written, press wires carried a story with a Washington dateline announcing a new $49,000 grant from the Department of Agriculture to the Oregon State University department of microbiology for a study of sourdough French bread. This bread, the item explained, was first used in San Francisco to feed the miners of the '49 gold rush, and the government would like to know how it was made.

Many alert readers of my outdoors column in the Portland *Oregonian* called or wrote to protest this "bureaucratic squandering of taxpayers' money" on a subject that had been covered by me many times in the past, and was available for just the price of a copy of the newspaper.

Not only that, but sourdough French bread did not originate in San Francisco, during the gold rush or any other time. The same product has been around for centuries.

Embarrassed OSU faculty members rushed into print with an official explanation of the "sourdough scandal," but despite the logical statement that this was merely part of a larger program of basic research in micro-organisms important to the dairy, meat, chemical, and other important industries, as well as to commercial bakeries, it was not likely that many readers were impressed—which may indicate that long-suffering taxpayers are getting a little fed up with the research grant racket, and are suggesting that a little common sense comes cheaper.

In any case, this book contains all the taxpayer and homemaker need know about the wondrous ways of sourdough, and it comes to you at considerably less than $49,000.

L'Affaire Sourdough puts me in mind of that delightful essay by Charles Lamb (1775-1834), *A Dissertation on Roast Pig*. This tale was purportedly discovered in an ancient Chinese scroll by Lamb, who worked as a clerk for the East India Company. For seventy thousand years, the story says, man ate his meat raw, clawing or biting it from his prey. All this changed in the Golden Age, which Confucious called *Cho-fang* or Cook's Holiday. It was kicked off by a lowly swineherd named Ho-ti one morning when he went to the woods to work, leaving his cottage in the care of his eldest son, Bo-bo, a lubberly boy who was fond of playing with fire.

Bo-bo set the cottage on fire, which roasted alive a newly farrowed litter of piglets. When Bo-bo tried to save them, knowing the wrath of his father, he burned his fingers. Instinctively putting his fingers in his mouth to soothe them, he tasted the exotic goodness of roast pork for the first time.

Returning to find his cottage in smoking ashes, and his idiot son feasting on the roasted piglets, Ho-ti whipped the boy, but accidentally burned his fingers on the hot pig, too. He rushed to the village to spread the word. The Celestial Court soon heard of it, and roast pork became a national fad. All the insurance companies went broke as people burned their houses down with pigs in them to partake of this new culinary

delight—called "home-cooked" porker—and the lubberly boy will forever be remembered by the slang word
boo-boo.

The origin of sourdough probably occurred in the
same accidental way, and probably long before roast
pig was invented.

In spite of its ancient origins, the art of sourdough
cookery is still considered complicated and even mysterious by some folks today. Those who have never
tasted a tangy sourdough biscuit or flapjack have a
treat in store for them. They will be hooked just like
Ho-ti and Bo-bo. Old-timers who grew up with a sourdough starter pot behind the stove back in the Good Old
Days, will find that when the first heady aroma per-
meates the house, their latent taste buds will be re-
juvenated, and they may go sailing away on a nostalgic journey to their boyhood days.

No one seriously claims you can eat your way to
health and happiness the sourdough way, or that sourdough will eventually save the world.

You'll have to judge that for yourself.

We can only guarantee you'll have fun finding out.

This collection of sourdough recipes had its genesis
on the North Dakota prairies where both my bride,
Myrtle, and I were born and raised. My parents had
come from the frontier woods region of Minnesota and
Wisconsin; hers hailed from County Down in North
Ireland, via Canada.

My mother came from a line of Pennsylvania Dutch
backwoodsmen, down through Ohio River and Iowa
pioneers and circuit riders. Her name was Minnie
and her twin sister was Mina. At age 13 they were left
motherless. Minnie went to work to bring in a little
cash, and Mina stayed home with the 11 smaller chil-

dren to look after the house. A mainstay of the home was the old sourdough pot behind the wood-fired range.

My grandfather on my father's side, a big, black-haired Swede immigrant to the Wisconsin frontier and the village blacksmith, lived on sourdough from a pot replenished almost daily beside the kitchen fireplace. He had reached the age of nearly 89 when, it was said, his wild living and women-chasin' done him in.

I practically grew up on sourdough flapjacks, bread, and hot biscuits made by my mother from the starter in the old butter crock, behind the kitchen range with the hot water reservoir. My parents lived to an advanced age, but as for me, there has been some discussion as to whether or not I've already outlived my usefulness.

Myrtle was one of four children born to Tom and Annie Tate who had immigrated to the bleak, unbroken prairies around Portal, N.D., during the big land boom to escape the drudgery and poverty of the Old Country.

For more than half a century they farmed that raw, unforgiving soil, through prosperous times, droughts, dust storms, soul-crushing depression, and grasshopper plagues. One of Myrtle's fondest memories of those close-knit family days "on the farm" was the uncanny instinct her mother had. Almost invariably she would set out an extra place at "dinnertime" as the noon meal was always called, for company. And almost invariably, just as they would sit down to the table, along would come the John Deere man, the Presbyterian minister, or a bachelor neighbor.

They all knew about Annie Tate's hot biscuits, Irish stews, and apple pies. And Annie knew they knew.

That's where Myrtle, like many a North Dakota farm gal, learned to cook—a happy circumstance that came in mighty handy when we were collecting and testing all these old and new recipes.

The people who came from the small towns of America or off farms, almost without exception, recall that sourdough—although it might not have been called that —was a part of their early memories. In my early years, after I had left home and worked at various jobs in the West and North country, almost invariably the cookshack had a sourdough pot working at all times. In Alaska I found sourdough so common that it was featured on the menu of every cafe and lunch counter.

The belief, however, that sourdough is only for backwoods trappers and prospectors is a wretched injustice, as you shall see. Sourdough cookery is an art that is equally at home in a camp, on a trail, or in your new all-electric kitchen.

To one who grew up on sourdough, the current revival of this lost art comes as no surprise—although the popularity and enthusiasm often reach startling proportions, inasmuch as this is one of the oldest forms of cooking known to man.

As Wildlife Editor of *The Oregonian* I occasionally fill a hole in the column on a dull winter day with an old-fashioned recipe from our collection picked up while roamin' around the mine camps, construction jobs, and logging "shows" of the West Coast and Alaska.

This always results in a fresh blaze of telephone calls and letters from readers pleading for more information. In fact, the response I get has become such a burden that I seldom run them any more. I simply can't handle the office burden in addition to regular writing chores.

On one of these occasions I published a formula for starter which had previously appeared in a chapter of my *Old-Fashioned Dutch Oven Cookbook* (The Caxton Printers, Ltd., Caldwell, $3.95) entitled "Cooking the Sourdough Way."

As a light-hearted spoof, I added that sourdough might save the world. The response indicated that a lot of readers took me seriously. At least 150 of them wrote in to tell me so, and a lot more called personally on the telephone.

Not long after that, a story appeared in *The Oregonian* under a Redmond dateline, about a lady named Mrs. Marcia Chase who had celebrated her 101st birthday. As usual, the reporter asked her to what she attributed her longevity.

"To keeping busy, staying decent, and eating sourdough bread," she replied.

In any case, sourdough cooking is back, and this time probably to stay.

Perhaps it's a symptom of nostalgic longing for the good old days. Perhaps people are turning around and taking a peek backward, to see if they have left behind some things of proven virtue and real value.

I dunno. Maybe sourdough will save the world.

We hope this modest cookbook will help you, too, on the Sourdough Way to happiness and health. All the following recipes are tried and proven. Some date all the way back to grandfather's farm in the Wisconsin backwoods. Others were collected along the way—in Alaska, in the camps, from friends and relatives. Some are originals. Myrtle not only furnished several superb creations of her own, but checked them all personally in the Holm kitchen.

Many of them have been adapted for use by the beginner as well as the experienced cook, working with simple ingredients and equipment found in any kitchen.

Some are adapted to use in camps and even on the trail.

As for me, I gave them all the severest confrontation possible—the taste and chew test. And, as I said, sourdough may save the world yet, if not the waistline.

DON HOLM
Beaverton, Oregon

THE COMPLETE
SOURDOUGH COOKBOOK

I

SOURDOUGH MAY SAVE THE WORLD

So what is *sourdough?*

No mystery. Sourdough is simply a home-grown "yeast factory" discovered by man not long after he learned how to pound roots or grind wild grain into a flour. Perhaps like Ho-ti and Bo-bo, some human-like progenitor was cooking a batch of flat cakes on a hot rock with a batter made of pounded grains and water in an earthen bowl, when a neighbor yelled, "the mastodons are migrating!" and everybody grabbed a spear and took after the winter's meat supply. By the time they all got back, days later, the fire under the flat rock was out, the cakes ruined, but the heat of the stones on which the earthen pot sat had kept the flour-and-water mixture warm, furnishing an ideal host for yeast spores which are everywhere in the air around us (and which, in fact, may be one of the secrets of life), and fermentation had taken place. To the hungry hunters, the aroma coming from the bubbling pot was heavenly (as they must have thought of heaven, that being another name for a full belly). Quickly building another fire, and not bothering to whip up a new batch of flour and water, they used the old bubbly stuff in the pot—and Eureka! They had discovered sourdough, made possible by the natural leavening process.

They also soon learned that this sourdough "starter" could be kept going indefinitely, provided they replenished what they took out of the pot with fresh flour and water and kept it at the proper degree of warmth so it would continue to "work" or ferment. They learned that this yeast factory could be "killed" by too much heat, and rendered dormant by cold (although in the latter case it could be brought back as soon as warmed again).

It has become popular today for self-styled connoisseurs of sourdough to announce great claims for longevity of starters. Usually these are supposed to be ancient "sponges" originated in Alaska where prospectors considered them more precious than the gold dust they sought. A number of Alaskan starters have been traced back through three generations, it is claimed. The House of Wickersham in Juneau has a starter that is supposed to have been working for forty-five years. Up in Fairbanks, where I spent a year or two in pre-war times, the granddaddy of them all has been going for seventy years, having come out of Dawson in the Yukon Territory in 1898.

In the old Alaskan days, sourdough was often kept in firkins, wooden pots bound with metal straps. Firkins could be transported without breaking as a butter crock would. Prospectors going in on foot, however, always carried the starter sponge buried in the top of the flour bag.

Jack Hines, in his autobiography, *Minstrel of the Yukon* (Greenberg: Publisher, N.Y., 1948), gives one version of how prospectors got their name: "A sourdough is a man who has spent at least one winter in the far North. There was no yeast in the Nome region, and the word developed from the old prospectors' habit of letting dough for flapjacks ferment by itself before use. Until a man became a sourdough, he was a *chechaquo*.

This is a Chinik word which is applied to migrant birds —birds which visit Alaska only in the warm summer months and fly south to greener lands in winter."

Neither his explanation of *sourdough* or *chechaquo* is accurate.

When man began to cultivate grain and grind it into flour for bread—the staple of all human societies—the yeast-making process was exactly the same as the way we make sourdough today. Ultimately, of course, the scientists of food chemistry came up with cheap and more convenient ways of manufacturing simple yeast.

In the sourdough yeast-making process, the yeast spores, given the proper host such as flour and warm water, break down the starch into sugar, the fermentation can continue as long as it has nutrients to feed on.

The role of sourdough or yeast in bread baking, of course, is primarily that of a leavening or "raising" agent which transforms the thick, unpalatable dough into a light-textured tasty and chewy baked product.

For some reason, modern bakeries—at least those which cater to the supermarket trade—simply can't mass-produce this kind of bakery goods. As a result, modern civilization is denied the goodness, the superior qualities of sourdough foods. A whole generation or two has grown up without even having tasted "real" bakery goods. Very few people remember that sourdough was the basis for all farm and pioneer cooking in the olden days. On the frontier, a sourdough starter (or sponge, as it is sometimes called) was the most important personal possession a family could have, next to the Holy Bible; it was something to be guarded at the expense of almost everything else, and many a tale has been told of this. The starter was the wellspring of every meal. From it one could not only make bread, biscuits, and flapjacks, but feed the dogs, treat burns and wounds, chink the log cabin, brew a form of hootch, and, some say, even re-sole one's boots.

No camp cooking was complete without sourdough. It fed generations of miners, trappers, mountain men, and pioneers—and later farm families, who could not have survived the rigors without it.

It was the mainstay of the "Cowboy West," and no chuckwagon would leave the home ranch for the round-up without a keg of starter and the "makin's." It became the *pièce de résistance* of the Basques who migrated to America from the mountain regions of the Spanish-French border to become the West's best sheep-herders, who baked the Sign of the Cross into every loaf of Dutch oven sourdough bread they made.

In recent years, thank heaven, the art of sourdough has been revived before it was killed by too much "civilization" just as yeast spores can be killed by too much heat. Many older folks are re-discovering it, and many young 'uns coming along are being introduced to its wonders, as well. Even a few self-conscious commercial bakeries are getting the message and offering sourdough sidelines, and now and then you come across a small bakery that even specializes in sourdough, or sheepherder or Basque breads, and people soon find out and come from far and near to patronize the place.

One thing is certain: once you have tasted and compared genuine sourdough bread, flapjacks, biscuits, and cakes with those semi-edible abominations you take home from the supermarket, you won't be the same again.

Any renaissance, of course, starts with a "starter," and this is what you make first. You've probably heard some of the Old Wives' (or Old Prospectors') tales about it. Be wary of entrepreneurs who try to sell you an "authentic sourdough starter," usually one purported to have come from an old Alaskan trapper who kept it goin' nigh onto sixty years. A good starter will keep for years if properly cared for, but in case you lose it, don't fret. It is as simple to make a new one as mixing flour and water.

Naturally, many folks are so proud of their starter pot they make a special effort to keep the continuity going. Miss Mary Rogers, of Mexico, Missouri, recently took me to task for making the above statements. Her starter, she said, has been going strong for seven years—and she has a reputation of being the best sourdough cook in Missouri.

And Mrs. David Ackerman of Prairie City, Oregon, wrote to us not long ago ". . . just to let you know we came across your sourdough recipe for cookies the other day, and my husband is now a *sourdough nut*. We have had our starter for four years and your recipes are the only ones (excluding the original pancake recipe we found our starter recipe with) that really works with our starter. We are also crazy about your waffle recipe you printed some time ago."

Mrs. A. G. Campbell of Medford, Oregon, was one of those readers who used a sourdough recipe from my column, but, she wrote, "I lost it and my cooking department hasn't been the same since!"

I sent her a duplicate.

Another reader, Mrs. Mary K. Edmundson of Hood River, Oregon, wrote for copies of my recipes for her daughter who lives in Hong Kong. "I suppose it is for use in her home, but it might introduce a new feature at the *Juno*, the revolving restaurant which her husband operates. One never knows!"

Mrs. Gabriel Lende of Pasco, Washington, also wrote for recipes because "My father was a real cowboy. Rode the rough string from Wyoming to Montana in 1900."

And a gent named Bill Hunter of Portland addressed a letter to me, "Dear Fishin' Liar! I tried some recipes you had in the paper and they were fab-u-lous! Happy hookin' an' shootin'!"

So, since everything begins with a simple starter, that's where we will begin too.

Maybe your grandchildren, years hence, can brag to their friends that they, too, have their own sourdough starter, handed down through the generations from the one you are about to begin right now.

II

GETTING STARTED WITH "STARTER"

JUST TO SHOW you how simple sourdough is, you're going to learn how to make a sourdough starter in less than 60 seconds:

Put 2 cups of flour into a crock, jar, or Tupperware bowl that is at least warm room temperature. Add 2½ cups lukewarm water, and set the whole batch in a warm but *not hot* place.

That's all there is to it.

This is your personal yeast "factory."

In about four or five days, the pot will be bubbling slowly, like one of those Yellowstone Park wonders, and an aroma which you have never experienced on this earth will fill your kitchen with a heady fragrance from the wine of gods.

Of course you can help it along a bit. You can use warm water that you've just boiled potatoes in; or you can sprinkle a package of active dry yeast over the flour before you mix in the plain warm water. That way you'll have a "starter" going in only a few hours all ready for business.

By this time you are probably as anxious as a Hillsboro, Oregon, lady who wrote: "For heaven's sake send me a copy of your recipes real soon please. I have some sourdough starter and does it smell good! What do I do next?

In spite of all the hocus-pocus that has been promoted and broadcast by fast-buckers—like those stories of starter being kept alive and handed down from generation to generation—there is absolutely nothing to sourdough starter but flour and water. While it is convenient to keep a starter going at all times, provided you use some and replenish what you use with fresh flour and water frequently, it can be kept for several weeks under refrigeration, and frozen for even longer. Just remember always to "bring it back" to room temperature so that it starts working again before using it in recipes.

My mother kept a batch going behind the kitchen stove all winter long, but if she accidentally lost one, it was a simple matter to start another. Today it is even more simple, as you will see.

The "starter" or "sponge" or whatever you call it is merely fermented water and flour, actively working —a homemade personal "yeast factory."

To elaborate a little: The first step in making a starter is obtaining a suitable container, such as a bean pot, butter crock if you can find one, or plastic bowl. Even a glass mason jar is okay, too, but never use a metal container. The bowl should be scalded before using to inhibit the growth of unwanted bacteria. On the trail, in the old Alaska and Klondike gold rush days, a starter "sponge" was kept right inside the bag of flour and then revived when camp was made and a fire going. In cold weather, starters lose some potency, but can be revived with a tablespoon of pure cider vinegar.

It is usually convenient to have a loose-fitting lid for the pot, to keep the dust, or perhaps the cat, out of the working starter; but the pot should never be tightly

Sourdough starter

closed because the mixture has to attract those yeast spores from the surrounding air, remember?

Even Henry David Thoreau, America's most famous hippie, had some thoughts about sourdough in his *Walden, or Life in the Woods.*

"Leaven," said Ralph, "which some deem the soul of bread, the spiritus which fills its cellular tissue, which is religiously preserved like the vestal fire—some precious bottleful, I suppose, first brought over in the Mayflower, did the business for America, and its influence is still rising, swelling, spreading, in cerealian billows over the land—this seed I regularly and faithfully procure from the village, till at length one morning I forgot the rules, and scalded my yeast."

I break off Thoreau at that point, where he starts to tell how he learned to get along without his starter after he lost it. He goes into detail about how he didn't want to carry this starter around in his pocket in a bottle anyway, which indicates how little he knew about it. Thoreau also reported he did not use any "sal-soda or any acid or alkali" in his bread. Instead he used the "recipe of Marcus P. Cato."

Marcus Porcius Cato recorded his recipe for bread about two centuries before Christ, as follows:

"Panem depsticium sic facito. Manus Mortariumque bene lavato. Farinam in mortarium indito, aquae paulatim addito, subigitoque pulchre. Ubi bene subegeris, definigito, coquitoque sub testu."

Which means: "Make kneaded bread thus. Wash your hands and trough well. Put the meal into the trough, add water gradually, and knead it thoroughly. When you have kneaded it well, mould it, and bake it under a cover."

You now know why the Roman Empire fell. You

also see Henry David Thoreau exposed for what he was
—a super-educated intellectual snob.

Nowhere was sourdough more appreciated in the
American West than in the cow camps and on the
ranches. Cowboys preferred sourdough bread to anything. They could stand baking powder biscuits in a
pinch, according to Andy Adams in his classic *Log of
a Cowboy*, and buttermilk biscuits were passable if a
pretty nester gal made 'em, but nothing compared to
his "sourdoughs." In comparison, the cowboys called
"baker's bread" wasp's nest or gun waddin'.

As a matter of fact, if it weren't for his Arbuckle
coffee, which the chuckwagon cook got in cloth bags in
green bean form and roasted in his Dutch oven, his
Eagle Brand milk, and his "sourdoughs," the West
would never have been won. Not all cowboys would
admit they liked the "canned cow," however. As Char-
lie Russell, the famed Montana artist, remarked about
Eagle Brand, "I think it must have come from a bird.
It's a cinch it never came from an animal with horns."

But then most cowboys were extremely sensitive
about their manhood, and drinking canned cow made
their breath smell like a new-born calf.

Later, when Carnation Milk came on the market
from its little plant in Kent, Washington, it was widely
accepted in the West. A ranch lady with a poetic bent
wrote to the company, in hopes of being rewarded, a
little ditty that went:

> *Carnation Milk is the best in the lan'*
> *Comes to the table in a little red can.*

When the cowboy mailman stopped by on his way to

the post office, she gave the verse to him. Before posting it, the cowboy added his own version:

Carnation Milk is the best in the lan'
Comes to the table in a little red can.
No teats to pull, no hay to pitch,
*Jus' punch a hole in the sonofabitch.**

As a matter of interest only, you might like to know how the old chuckwagon cook and the rendezvous "camp robbers" made their sourdough batter. The container was usually a nine-gallon Hudson's Bay Company high wine keg or the equivalent. Into it went five quarts of flour, some salt, and lukewarm water to make a batter. The keg was set by the fireplace or out in the warm sun to ferment for a couple of days. Some added pieces of raw potato, raw sugar or molasses, pickle juice, or vinegar to make it "work" faster.

If it were a new keg, the first batch was dumped out or used to chink the logs of the cabin, and a new batch started in the now-seasoned container. In the winter the cook took the keg to bed with him. In any case, the starter was minded carefully in order to keep the fermentation going. When it was ready to use, the cook always replaced what was taken out with fresh flour and water.

I have found among my readers considerable confusion over the use of yeast in sourdough cooking. Yeast is a modern innovation. The original sourdough did not use it—in fact, *made* it. Nowadays we use it to speed up things a bit, and the same goes for baking soda or baking powder.

---

*Ramon F. Adams, *Come An' Get It* (University of Oklahoma Press, 1952).

If you want real old-time sourdough, do not use yeast. The less yeast used, the richer and headier the sourdough, but the longer it takes and the trickier the recipes are. For example, real sourdough bread does not have any yeast in either the starter or the bread dough mix. Neither does sourdough French bread, but the latter is almost too difficult to handle in the average home kitchen, so recipes have been developed using yeast. Some French bread recipes take as long as 24 hours to complete.

This is also a good place to mention that today there is a healthy trend—and I use the term deliberately— back to good old stone-ground flour, to rye flour, corn-meal, wheat germ, and quick oats, as substitutes for store-bought flour. These can be obtained from gourmet shops and health food stores, and in some of the bigger supermarkets. They are much tastier and more nutritious, but do require a little more care.

Some secrets of good sourdough cooking are:

—Avoid mixing the batter too much. Over-mixing knocks the gases out of the dough, which are needed for the raising process.

—Sourdough cooking requires slightly more heat or a longer cooking time than ordinary baking.

—Never put back in the starter pot anything but flour or water, especially no sugar, salt, eggs, soda, or cooking oil. If starter turns orange, throw it away!

—Use lukewarm water, never hot or cold water.

Remember sourdough bread and pastries can be kept indefinitely in your freezer; they even improve with age!

—Baking soda turns sourdough yellow, so you may wish to use baking powder instead.

—Wheat flour in starter doesn't raise as high but works faster than white.

—The batter should always be at room temperature when you use it. When making starter, first warm the pot with hot water.

—Buttermilk usually requires a bit more leavening when used in most recipes.

—Sourdough is amazingly versatile, and can be adapted to many recipes.

You will find that all the recipes in this book have been adapted to modern home cooking, as well as camp cooking. Today folks don't have a kitchen range "banked" for the night, for example. Moreover, I have found that most readers want to get at it right away. They don't want to have to let things "set" for hours or days, as was necessary in times past. So there are all kinds of tricks and shortcuts you can use, such as a good pre-mixed flapjack flour combined with sourdough, which gives you all the taste and pleasures of authentic sourdough flapjacks without so much of the fuss and bother.

As a kid just out of high school, back in the Dirty Thirties, one of the most unforgettable characters in my perambulations around the world was a guy named Harvey up in Juneau. He was the first person I met when I got off the northbound steamship at the tail end of October (when everyone else was heading for the "outside"). I had about ten *centavos* left after matching my skill and luck against members of the ship's crew in the steerage section of the old *SS Alaska*. I also had a five-dollar sleeping bag, and no place to unroll it. Harvey had just moved into town for the winter from his claim on Atlin Lake. His "town house" was a one-room wannigan just outside Juneau on the road to the Mendenhall Glacier. He let me spread my bag on the floor for a couple of weeks until I got settled, and also stuffed me daily with all manner of goodies made from a vile-looking crock of sourdough he kept behind the stove.

He made almost everything we ate out of that crock. And each time he made a pilgrimage to it, he would lovingly replace what he borrowed with fresh flour and water, and often the leavin's of the last meal. The pot had a green slime around the edges and the contents floated a layer of pure alcohol which looked as deadly as carbolic acid. But Harvey scoffed at any suggestion his sourdough starter could be a mite unsanitary or unhealthy. He said he'd been born and brought up on sourdough and expected to go on using it until the Northern Lights went out.

He was about seventy-five or eighty then, and the last I heard tell, he had lived to be about ninety-nine when he died an alcoholic.

A starter should be used and replenished at least once a week—oftener would be better. In between you can keep it in a covered bowl in the refrigerator, or it can be frozen and kept indefinitely. There is a powdered or dehydrated starter now available commercially, in packets handy for hikers and campers, which needs no refrigeration. I don't know how this is prepared, but would assume that it is nothing more than flour, dry yeast, and possibly some sugar, mixed dry. Then when ready to use, you activate it with lukewarm water and let it start working.

The first time I saw a batch of sourdough, that I was conscious of, was when my dad took me to the funeral of his father at the old pioneer homestead in northern Wisconsin. I was about nine at the time. Behind the stove in the kitchen lean-to was a one-gallon crock that had come over with my forebears from Sweden, and in it was a yeasty mixture that filled the kitchen with fumes like a brewery. Around the rim of the crock the slime and scum had gathered like moss on an old hemlock.

When I wrinkled up my nose, my dad told me this was a sourdough starter that had been cooking since he was a little boy, always replenished after every use with leftover batter and scraps. To me it looked like a garbage disposal. I marveled that anyone could eat it and survive—and I suspect now that my dad was perpetuating the same old hoary legend about sourdough starters.

Although a starter is simply flour and water, there are a number of ways folks make it—and, in fact, most sourdough cooks develop their own individual idiosyncrasies about it. I'll list some of these for you, so you can take your own choice:

No. 1—The formula we use is simply 2 cups of flour with a package of dry yeast stirred in, and enough lukewarm water to make a thick batter. I stir it only enough to break up the lumps, then let stand in a warm place for at least 24 hours or until the house is filled with a delectable yeasty odor.

No. 2—Mix 2 cups of flour with enough lukewarm water to form a thick batter, and let stand uncovered for four or five days, or until it begins working. This basic recipe requires a carefully scalded container.

No. 3—Same as above but use warm milk instead of water. One reader told me she took the milk right out of the cow, but a real warm cow might be hard to come by these days.

No. 4—Boil some potatoes for supper, save the potato water, and use it lukewarm with flour to make a thick batter without the yeast. This is a good way to make it in camp, where you have no yeast available and want fast results. This is also the way most farm gals made it in the olden days. Let stand a day or so, or until it smells right.

No. 5—Here's another variation: mix 4 cups flour, 2 tablespoons salt, 2 tablespoons sugar, 4 cups lukewarm potato water in a crock or jar and let stand in a warm place uncovered for several days. This one is *my* last choice, but for some strange reason it, or variations of it, can be found in practically every corner of the land.

No. 6—Here's a good milk starter: let a cup or so of milk stand for a day or so in an uncovered container at room temperature. Then add a cup of flour, mix, and let stand for another couple of days or until it starts working, after which it is ready to use.

It takes several hours for yeast plants to start growing under ideal conditions, which is from 75 degrees to about 90. If the house is cold, you might try using a mildly warm oven for a few minutes at a time, but be careful it doesn't get too hot and kill the spores.

If you keep the starter in the refrigerator between times, take it out several hours in advance of using it, until it is again at room temperature and active. Then, always remember to replenish in the pot, the starter you remove for cooking purposes. Do this by adding enough flour and lukewarm water to restore the mixture to its original amount and consistency. Let this work in the pot for at least a day, before storing it in the refrigerator.

After running one of the basic starter recipes in my

newspaper column, I received a letter from a Warren, Oregon, lady who wrote:

"I was so pleased to hear of your sourdough cookbook that I am ready to give it another try. My last starter blurped itself to death in lonely agony while I was on an unplanned weekend trip. The dear thing crept over, between, behind and under drainboard, stove and wall looking for help, before it finally dried up (but didn't blow away!).

"Perhaps I'll remember to use a *large* bowl hereafter."

Another convert to sourdough was an 85-year-old retired gentleman living at Seaside, Oregon. He wrote:

"At Seaside we have several genuine Alaskan sourdoughs and really, while they talk a lot about sourdough, I don't think any of them know how to make it. I intend to use your recipes and do a little experimenting, and then invite them all in for a feast."

Mrs. Alta Boyes of Newberg, Oregon, sent me a letter about her adventures:

"Dear Don: I hear you have a boat called *Sourdough*. Well, I can go you one better. One night I was making some sourdough biscuits and put my head in the oven to see if they were done. I smelled something burning. I thought it was the biscuits, but it was only my *wig*, which I now call 'Old Sourdough'!"

I guess I started something when I named my two boats *Wee Sourdough* and *Wild Sourdough*.

Well, now you've got your own starter going, and have been thoroughly steeped in the legends and traditions of the sourdough cooking arts.

It's time to see what else is cookin'.

You will find that most recipes in this book call for

about half a cup of starter or sponge, actively working, as the basis for the recipe. Sometimes, little variations in results come from variations in the way the ingredients are put together. In most cases, the steps given are those which worked out best for us. They may not be the *only* way, or the *best* way for you in your kitchen; but they will give you a good starting point from which to begin. You will note, too, as you gain experience, that different brands of the same ingredients often cause variations in results.

Now you are on your own, and you will encounter frequent variations caused by your individual conditions, but don't be alarmed or disappointed if things don't work out exactly as described here. If you start with these, you won't go wrong, and chances are you'll find ways of improving them or adapting them to your own individual talents and inspirations.

That is one of the delights of sourdough cooking. That and sampling the end product.

III

THE EASY ONES TO LEARN BY

FLAPJACKS AND sourdough are inseparable handmaidens. When you mention one, you can't help but think of the other. As old Harv used to tell me, the Lord put flapjacks on this earth just to show man what Paradise was all about, but first He created sourdough, just so's a man could make flapjacks.

Flapjacks probably originated with the primitive flat mealy cakes cooked on hot stones that are still a universal way of making a meal in many backwoods parts of the world. For some reason, many housewives today—and even many cooking experts, as I have learned to my amazement—don't know the difference between hotcakes, pancakes, and flapjacks. There is no difference. They are all one and the same; it's just that when you speak of flapjacks, you are generally speaking of *sourdough* flapjacks.

Flapjacks were not as large a part of the cowboy's menu as were sourdough biscuits and breads, especially on the trail or at the roundups. Flapjacks were just too much bother to make under chuckwagon conditions, and besides, cowboys always got up before breakfast and were out on the range before their juices began working.

As Teddy Roosevelt recorded from his days as a rancher in the North Dakota Badlands:

"In the morning the cook is preparing breakfast

Sourdough flapjacks

long before the first glimmer of dawn. As soon as it is
ready, probably about 3 o'clock, he utters a long-drawn
shout, and all the sleepers feel it is time to be up on the
instant, for they know there can be no such thing as
delay on the roundup, under penalty of being set afoot.
Accordingly, they bundle out, rubbing their eyes and
yawning, draw on their boots and trousers—if they
have taken the latter off—roll up and cord their bed-
ding, and usually without any attempt at washing,
crowd over to the little smoldering fire, which is placed
in a hole dug in the ground, so that there may be no
risk of it spreading. The men are rarely very hungry
at breakfast, and it is a meal that has to be eaten in the
shortest order, so it is perhaps the least important.
Each man, as he comes up, grasps a tin cup and a plate
from the mess-box, pours out his tea or coffee, with
sugar, but of course no milk, helps himself to one or
two of the biscuits that have been baked in a Dutch
oven, and perhaps also to a slice of the fat pork swim-
ming in the greases of the frying-pan, ladles himself
some beans, if there are any, and squats down on the
ground to eat his breakfast. . . ."*

The soldiers on the frontier during the Indian Wars
fared even worse than cowboys in the victuals department, although when a detail of cavalry happened upon
a wagon train bound for Oregon or California, there
was sure to be much bargaining with the womenfolks
for sourdough cakes and biscuits, and cold pancakes
which, sprinkled with sugar or molasses, were delicious
snacks for the trail.

As the *Soldier's Handbook* written by one N. Hersh-

*Theodore Roosevelt's *Ranch Life and the Hunting Trail*, illustrated
by Frederic Remington (New York: The Century Company, 1888 and
1915).

ler (Government Printing Office, 1884) pointed out,
"Disease and often death is the result of bad and illy-
prepared food; therefore it is of vital importance to
every soldier to know this useful art." Cooking, that
is. However, soldiers then, as now, were not likely to
be much impressed by "handbooks" written by Washington bureaucrats for their guidance.

Anyway, what I started to say was, sourdough flapjacks flourished more in the settlements, on the farms,
and in the winter quarters of trappers and prospectors,
and the logging camps of Michigan, Minnesota, and the
Pacific Northwest, than under field conditions.

And it doesn't take much travel through the camps
of Alaska, British Columbia, and the Western states
to reach the conclusion that there are about as many
flapjack recipes as there are flapjack fanciers. Here
are some we've licked our chops over, but you can draw
your own conclusions:

No. 1—Mix ½ cup active starter, ½ cup pancake
mix, 1 egg, 1 tablespoon cooking oil, ½ cup milk, ½
teaspoon soda. Lightly grease a hot griddle. Drop onto
griddle with a large spoon while the batter is still rising.

No. 2—Mix 1 cup starter, 1 cup flour, 1 egg, 2 tablespoons cooking oil, ¼ cup instant or evaporated milk.
Blend in 1 teaspoon salt, 1 teaspoon soda, 2 tablespoons
sugar. Let mixture bubble and foam a minute, then
drop spoonfuls onto hot griddle.

No. 3—Mix 2 cups starter, 2 cups flour, and 1 teaspoon baking soda, 2 well-beaten eggs or 1 tablespoon
powdered eggs, 1 tablespoon sugar, 1 teaspoon salt.
Stir in 2 or 3 tablespoons bacon fat, butter, or suet, and
cook on hot griddle.

No. 4—Mix 1 cup buttermilk pancake mix, ½ cup

starter, ½ cup milk, 1 egg, 1 tablespoon cooking oil, ½ teaspoon baking powder. Let stand a few moments, then drop onto hot griddle. (Berries can be added to any of these recipes.)

No. 5.—Beat 3 eggs. Add 1 cup sweet milk and 2 cups sourdough starter. Sift 1¾ cups all-purpose flour with 1 teaspoon soda, 2 teaspoons baking powder, 1½ teaspoons salt, ¼ cup sugar. Combine everything. Drop or spoon dough onto a greased griddle; or if an ungreased griddle is used, add ¼ cup melted fat to the batter. Test griddle for proper temperature by flicking a drop of water onto it. If it bounds off slowly, the heat level is right.

No. 6—This is an old-time flapjack recipe which was often cooked in a cast iron skillet over an open fire, and makes thin Swedish type cakes with a delicious nutty flavor and aroma. It uses a wheat flour starter, or part wheat flour (wheat flour can be added to any flapjack recipe for good results).

Make a good flapjack batter the night before, using a cup of starter, a couple of cups of flour, and warm water, and set in a warm place until morning. In the morning simply stir up the batter a little (not too much!) while the griddle is heating, adding:

¼ cup dry skim milk
2 tsps. salt
2 tsps. sugar

⅓ cup melted shortening
2 eggs, beaten
1 tsp. baking soda dissolved in warm water and added just before spooning the batter

No. 7—Mrs. Verne Peterson of Hillsboro, Oregon, after obtaining a starter recipe from me, sent the following for sourdough pancakes, which she said came from an elderly lady in Atlantic City:

First you make the starter with ¼ yeast cake, 1 teaspoon sugar, 1½ cups water and flour to make a soft sponge. Let set a day in a stone crock. At night add ½ quart water, ⅔ cup sugar, 1 teaspoon salt and flour enough to make a soft sponge.

In the morning put all but 1½ cups of it in a bowl (what you save, put back in the crock for more starter). Add 2 eggs, 1 tablespoon baking powder, 1 teaspoon soda. Don't have it too thick. Don't cut down on the sugar, as that is what makes it good."

So you pays your money and takes your choice. But just one more thing—for fluffy pancakes, fold in stiffly beaten egg whites just before baking on the griddle. This little trick will often make the difference between delicious 'cakes and superb ones.

We use a wheat germ flour or whole wheat flour, or cornmeal, as well as stone-ground flours in our sourdough starter occasionally to vary the results. The whole wheat, particularly, gives the hotcakes a distinctively different flavor.

If we make too many flapjacks for immediate use (a situation that seldom arises, however), we keep the leftovers in the refrigerator for later snacks. Sprinkled with sugar and cinnamon, or spread with cheese, honey, or even peanut butter and then rolled up, they are a favorite. This was as good as candy to frontier children, who most often had only backstrap molasses to spread on them. The cowboys called molasses "lick" or "long sweetenin'."

The many franchised "pancake houses" that seem to be a product of modern eating habits, usually offer a menu with an array of pancakes to dazzle the eye and reel the mind. Most of them are merely variations of the basic flapjack or pancake recipe, with fruit added, or the size changed in some way, such as "dollar pancakes" and "Swedish pancakes," and so on. You can duplicate any of them with a good sourdough flapjack batter, and we will leave this to your own devices and go on to the waffles.

You might think that waffles had no place in a camp cook's repertoire, but when they're made out of sourdough batter, I'll guarantee that Cookie will bring a waffle iron next time with the chuckwagon or pack-train—provided he can find an extension cord long enough.

Not long after I published my favorite waffle recipe in my column in *The Oregonian*, a Newberg, Oregon, lady wrote to tell me she was a retired schoolteacher who was "legally blind," but could see well enough to look for my sourdough recipes. She complained, however, that she was in trouble after 42 years of blissful married life. She had mislaid the recipe right after her husband had tasted his first sourdough waffle.

I rushed her a copy by fast pony express, and this is what it was:

Beat well 2 eggs, mix with ¼ cup cooking oil, ½ cup milk, 1 cup buttermilk pancake and waffle mix, ½ teaspoon baking powder, ½ cup sourdough starter.

Spoon the mixed batter in the usual way onto your waffle iron, preheated to the recommended temperature, and close the lid. When it quits steaming, it's done. Serve with maple syrup, berries and whipped cream, warm applesauce, or use the waffle as the base for creamed seafood, or chipped beef. This batch makes 10 to 12 waffle squares.

Don't hesitate to make as many as you feel like. You can freeze what you don't eat right away, and later

Sourdough waffles

take them out of the freezer and pop them in the toaster. You'll find them just as delicious as ever.

I must warn you about one precaution, however. Be sure to secure the lid of the waffle iron carefully. These waffles are so light they might float away when your back is turned.

Here's another one, not using the pre-mix pancake and waffle flour:

Beat 2 egg whites and yolks separately and set the frothy whites aside. Then mix 2 cups sourdough starter, ¼ cup dry skim powdered milk, ½ teaspoon salt, ½ teaspoon baking powder, ½ teaspoon soda, 1 tablespoon sugar, egg yolks, and ¼ cup cooking oil. As the last step, fold in the egg whites and mix quickly, then drop onto grates.

Miss Mary Rogers, the sourdough cooking champion of Mexico, Missouri, sent me her favorite waffle recipe:

½ cup sourdough starter	¾ tsp. baking soda, dissolved
1 cup milk	in a little warm water
1¼ cups flour	½ tsp. salt
1 egg, separated	¼ tsp. cream of tartar
4 tbsps. oleo, melted	1 tbsp. sugar

"At bedtime make a batter of the sourdough starter, milk and flour; cover and let set overnight if wanted for breakfast. It can be mixed early of a morning and set in a warm place if wanted for noon or evening. When the batter is very light, stir in the remaining ingredients, except the white of the egg and cream of tartar. Add cream of tartar to egg white, beat until stiff, then fold in last. Let batter set 20 or 30 minutes. Bake on hot waffle iron five to six minutes. Makes four waffles. This also makes good hotcakes."

Right here while you are between batches of sourdough flapjacks and waffles, I might record the fact that corn was the first ingredient used in the making of these delectable cakes. Since the Mayans, Aztecs, or Incas—no one knows which—invented or first cultivated corn or maize, both forms of cakes probably originated in the Western Hemisphere.

While pre-Columbian scholars today still marvel over the impact upon civilization that the development of corn caused, the ancient Mayans and Aztecs probably prepared their cakes thus:

The dried corn was soaked overnight to loosen the hulls. Then it was ground with stones, and mixed with water to form a paste. This was poured on a hot flat cooking stone, and in this way the pancake or flapjack was born.

History tells us also that since the year A.D. 1445, the day before Ash Wednesday, or Shrove Tuesday, has been proclaimed Pancake Day in Great Britain. Shriving cakes, as they were then called, were to be eaten by sinners who were confessed and thus shriven of their transgressions. The shriving cakes were, in other words, religious symbols. The flour was the staff of life, the salt the wholesomeness of the mother oceans; the eggs were for the Lenten Spirit, and milk was for innocence.

In Olney, in Merrie Olde England, they even held pancake races, which I believe is a custom that continues to this day. The races are run by women, each holding a griddle on which she must flip a pancake three times during the race.

In the early West, as we have seen, flapjacks were the breakfast staple in the camps, if not out on the trail. The lumber camps especially appreciated flapjacks. In the legendary camp of Paul Bunyan, the flapjack batter was made in a concrete mixer and the griddle greased by the cook skating around it with hams tied to his feet.

Today, flapjacks or pancakes are made in practically every country, civilized or otherwise. Whether you call them *tortillas*, *crêpes*, *plattar*, *blini*, *ableskivers*, *eier kuchen und pferden*, *palatcsinta*, *cannelloni*, or egg rolls, you are getting a local version of the ancient Mayan corn cake.

IV

BY BREAD ALONE

"MON DIEU!" exclaimed our Canadian fishing guide several years ago on a wilderness fishing trip, when we showed him how to make sourdough French bread in return for taking us into one of his secret Kamloops trout lakes. "You call eet sourdough *French* bread? Why ees this?"

Well, says I. We taught the Chinese how to make chop suey, the Mexicans how to make chili, the Germans how to make baloney, and the Italians how to make spaghetti—why not show the French how to make French bread?

I didn't mention that one thing the Hudson's Bay Company *voyageurs* liked better than parched corn, high wine, and Cree belles, was the kind of bread the "wintering partners" made on the post with a self-leavening dough (i.e., sourdough starter).

Nowadays, we make it exactly the way the cooks for the "Company of Adventurers" did two hundred years ago. Only much better, *cheri*.

It was sourdough French bread that made San Francisco famous, and that cosmopolitan city remains today the capital of French bread baking. However, the word has spread over much of the provinces, and here and there you will find a specialty bakery in some unlikely place that puts out a tasty product.

To be perfectly frank about it, sourdough French

bread is the most difficult and time-consuming of all sourdough cookery. It requires much care and patience, and occupies up to 24 hours in the process. It is, more-over, a challenge, and the more experience you acquire, the more expert you will become.

Because it is so difficult, we have tried to simplify where possible, to make the recipe better adapted to home conditions.

Sourdough French Bread—I

Dissolve a package of dry yeast in 1½ cups luke-warm water; mix with 1 cup sourdough starter in a large bowl, adding 4 cups flour, 2 tablespoons sugar, 2 teaspoons salt. Cover with a cloth and let rise in a warm place until doubled in size.

Then mix a cup of flour and ½ teaspoon of baking soda and stir this into the dough, adding enough flour to make a stiff dough. Knead on a flour-dusted board, until smooth and shiny. This kneading is the secret of good bread.

Shape the dough into half-loaf sizes, place on greased paper or sheet sprinkled with cornmeal, and leave in warm place until again double in size. Brush the top lightly with cold water, make a sharp slash about ¼ inch deep in top of loaf, and bake in a 400° oven. Place a shallow pan with a little hot water on the oven bottom. Bake until dark almond brown. Brush with melted but-ter and hot water, and then crisp in oven for 3 to 5 minutes.

Glaze, if desired, with a mixture of canned cow or fresh cream and egg yolk.

You will note that some commercial yeast is used in the above recipe (as in many other sourdough recipes in this book), in addition to the starter. This shortens

French bread

rise time, and makes it possible to start eating the hot fresh bread hours before you would have with the old original recipe. The starter, of course, gives the bread that delectable sourdough flavor. Moreover, it assists with the kneading process, making it possible for all the ingredients to be mixed in a large bowl at once. It helps to use a small amount of salad oil on your hands before kneading.

Sourdough French Bread—II

Here's another approach, for the serious experimenter to try:

Dissolve 1 package of active dry yeast in ¼ cup warm water. Combine this with 4½ cups unsifted flour, 2 tablespoons sugar, 2 teaspoons salt, 1 cup water, ½ cup milk, 2 tablespoons vegetable oil, and ¼ cup sourdough starter.

Mix and knead lightly and place in greased bowl to rise until double. Turn out onto floured board and divide dough into two parts. Shape dough parts into oblongs and then roll up tightly, beginning with one side. Seal outside edge by pinching and shape into size wanted. Place loaves on greased baking sheet and let rise until double again. Bake at 400° for about 25 minutes, after first slashing diagonal cuts on top, and brushing with water.

Sourdough French Bread—III

This was the old Alaskan way of making it, but it is heavier than most folks nowadays are used to. It does have the true authentic sourdough taste and smell, though. The starter must be lively and fresh. If it isn't help it along with a small amount of dry yeast before using.

1 cup starter	2 tbsps. melted shortening
½ cup milk	2 tsps. salt
1 tbsp. sugar	2½ cups flour

Mix ingredients in the above order, working in the flour a little at a time. Let dough rise in greased bowl until doubled. Knead again and form into French loaf. Cut cross-hatches on the top and let rise again. Bake at 325° for a half hour or until done. Brush top with butter.

Sourdough French rolls can also be made with the above recipes, simply by breaking or cutting off small pieces and shaping into roll sizes, allowing for room to double as they rise. The rolls can also be glazed just like the bread loaves, and also can be frozen for later use.

Progressing to easier, but just as rewarding, things, we come to plain sourdough bread, of which there are innumerable variations, just as there are innumerable flapjack recipes.

This one comes from a doctor we know who, between patients, goes upstairs to his private kitchen and relaxes with sourdough.

Over the years he has perfected a number of recipes which have warmed the hearts and innards of friends and patients alike. Here is one that is just what the doctor ordered.

The Doctor's Sourdough Bread

1 cup sourdough starter	¼ cup honey
2 cups warm water	7 cups all-purpose flour
2 cups warm milk	¼ cup wheat germ
1 tbsp. butter	2 tbsps. sugar
1 pkg. dry yeast	2 tsps. salt
2 tsps. baking soda	

Mix starter and 2½ cups of the flour and all the water the night before. Next morning mix butter with warm milk, and stir in yeast until dissolved. Add honey, and when thoroughly mixed, add 2 more cups flour, and stir in the wheat germ.

Sprinkle sugar, salt, and baking soda over the mixture. Gently press into dough and mix lightly. Allow to stand from 30 to 50 minutes until mixture is bubbly. Add flour until dough cannot be stirred, then place on floured board and knead 100 times or until silky mixture is developed. Form into four 1-pound loaves, place in well-greased loaf pans, size 9x2¾, and let rise until double—about 2 or 3 hours in a warm room.

Then bake in a hot oven at 400° for 20 minutes. Reduce oven temperature to 325° and bake 20 minutes longer or until thoroughly baked. Then remove from pans and place on rack to cool. Butter top of loaves to prevent too much crustiness.

An older sourdough bread recipe is this one handed down through the mining camps and trappers' rendezvous in Alaska for decades:

Alaskan Sourdough Bread

1 cup sourdough starter	1 tbsp. or 1 pkg. dry yeast
2½ cups warm water	1 tsp. baking soda
4 tbsps. melted lard	1 tbsp. salt
½ cup sugar	8 cups flour (approximately)

Combine ingredients, adding flour gradually, and knead until dough is smooth. Place in greased bowl in a warm place and let rise. When double, knead it down again and once more let rise. Then shape into loaves

Pumpernickel; French bread; Sheepherder bread; English muffins

and bake in moderate oven (about 375°) for about an hour or until done.

Sourdough Camp Bread

This one is for the rough-and-ready outdoorsman and is simple to make:

To 4 cups of starter add a mixture of 1 tablespoon of melted fat, bear grease, or shortening, 1 cup flour, 1 teaspoon baking powder. Keep adding flour until no more can be absorbed. Form into loaves. Put in greased pan and allow to stand until loaves have doubled in size, then bake.

Trapper's Sourdough Bread

2 cups sourdough starter	2 tbsps. sugar
4 cups flour	1 tsp. salt
	2 tbsps. shortening or fat

Mix the flour, salt, and sugar and scoop a hollow in it. Pour in the melted shortening and blend it with the sourdough starter inside the hollow. Then stir the whole into a soft batter. Add flour if too moist; or milk or water if too dry. Knead well but don't let the gases escape. Bang it around as fast as possible and break off loaf-sized chunks. Let rise until doubled in size, punch down, then bake in greased pans for about an hour in a moderate oven, after 15 minutes at a slightly hotter initial temperature. Baking should result in doubling the size again, and the loaves should turn out crispy brown.

Tip: For breads and biscuits, a very vigorous starter should be used. If necessary, make a new one.

Oatmeal Date Bread

1¼ cups sifted flour	¾ cup rolled oats
1½ tsps. baking powder	1 tsp. grated lemon peel
1 tsp. salt	¾ cup buttermilk
½ tsp. baking soda	2 eggs, beaten
¾ cup brown sugar,	¼ cup vegetable oil
firmly packed	½ cup sourdough starter

Sift flour, baking powder, soda, and salt together. Take 1 cup pitted dates, cut fine, and coat with 1 table-spoon of the flour mixture; then add to the remaining dry ingredients the brown sugar, the oats, and the lemon peel.

Blend the liquid ingredients and add all at once to flour mixture. Stir in the sourdough starter until everything is completely moistened. Pour into greased or wax-paper-lined loaf pan about 9x5. Bake at 350° for one hour. Allow to stand 10 minutes. Remove from pan and cool. Wrap in foil or plastic wrap and place in refrigerator. Spread with butter or cream cheese. This can also be toasted.

Sourdough Sheepherder Bread

Someday, if you are passing through the dusty cattle, mining, and gambling frontier town of Winnemucca, Nevada, on the meandering Humboldt River—made famous by the Applegate Party and other covered wag-on pioneers—tarry a moment, park the car, and walk down the main street toward the railroad tracks. You'll come to one of Nevada's most famous hostelries, the Winnemucca Hotel. This old-fashioned combination saloon, gambling joint, and cowtown inn for years was the gathering place for the Basques of that region. Here they ate in traditional style with long tables and longer reach. Upstairs, the sheepherders flopped their bedrolls after months out on the desert or in the mountains with the herds. Around the oilcloth-covered card tables, the herders relaxed over a game of *mus*, an old Basque-style poker game.

And, for years, this hostelry was famous not only for its wholesome family-style dinners, but also for its sourdough bread.

The first Basques came to America in the mid-1800s, landing mostly in the West at a time when gold fever was upon the land and mining camps were springing up like crocus flowers. They came from their homeland on the border between Spain and France, an ethnic group with a tongue unrelated to any other European language.

Coming from a mountain country and with a long tradition and instinct for raising domestic animals, they naturally gravitated to the open ranges of the American cattle and sheep regions.

Today, there are about 60,000 Basques in the western part of the U.S., including the original immigrants and their descendants and the current numbers who come here on three-year work permits. They are so skilled in animal husbandry and so essential to the modern sheep and cattle-raising industry, that special immigration rules were written for them. They are not all sheepherders, of course. Descendants of the early immigrants can be found in all the professions and types of business enterprises—Nevada has had at least one governor of Basque descent—throughout the West.

But in the old places like Jordan Valley, Oregon, and Winnemucca, there still remain colorful traces of the old life, and out on the lonely deserts, in the high meadows of the Rocky Mountains, and down in the hot reaches of Hells Canyon, the Basque sheepherder still holds forth with his faithful dogs and unique Gypsy wagon (probably the forerunner of today's pickup camper).

And in these lonely camps you still find the Basque herder baking his sourdough bread by means of the old cast iron camp Dutch oven buried in coals.

You will note, too, if you ever are fortunate enough to visit a Basque sheepherder's camp, that each of the golden loaves rising in the Dutch ovens has the Sign of the Cross as well as the imprint of the cast iron cover on its top. The Dutch oven is strictly an American invention, but the Sign of the Cross came about this way according to legend:

Once an outlaw sneaked into a herder's camp and put cyanide, used on the range for killing coyotes, into the herder's sourdough pot. When the herder returned to make his sourdough bread, something impelled him to scratch the Sign on the top of the loaf with his knife. The same instinct compelled him to give the first piece of the hot fresh bread to his dog, thus saving his own life. Ever since then Basques have put the Sign of the Cross on the top of their loaves. I have even heard of Dutch oven covers being cast with the Sign on the inside so that the bread rises into the mark; but I have yet to find one of these rare collector's items.

The sheepherder, out on the range, eats only twice a day. At first light of dawn he is out of his bedroll and splashing cold water on his face, if he is camped by a spring. For breakfast he will break off crusts of sourdough bread made the day before, and wash them down with hot coffee mixed about half and half with canned cow. Before leaving for the day he will prepare a new batch of sourdough bread.

When he returns in the evening, the sourdough bread, which has been baking in the buried oven all day, will be ready. As the hot sun drops behind the range and the distant mountains are painted with afterglow, he will prepare an omelet of bacon and potatoes, partake of the fresh hot bread, and wash everything down with strong wine squirted into his mouth from a goatskin *bota*. Then he will stretch out on his bedroll, gaze up at the star-twinkled sky, and listen to the sounds of the night mixed with the bleating of lambs and the tinkling of the belled leaders.

If you are outdoors, you can make yours the way he made his bread:

Dig a two-foot hole in the ground and build a roaring fire in the morning; when it has burned down to coals, prepare the bread dough. Load the Dutch oven, bury it in the coals, put on the lid, and shovel coals on top. Then cover the whole ball of wax with dirt. When you return at night it is ready to eat and finger-lickin' fresh.

The original Basque sheepherder bread was always made in a Dutch oven, with the starter kept in a keg or crock with a tight lid. The batter was made by digging a hole in a panful of flour and filling the hole with a handful of starter, working the flour into it from the edges, all the time mixing in a little salt and baking soda. When enough flour was added to make a soft dough, it was then flattened out into the Dutch oven, after the latter had first been pre-heated in the coals. The oven was then bedded back on the coals and covered with the lid, and more coals piled on top. It was then covered with dirt if one were going to be out in the hills all day. It could, of course, be tended during the baking period, and fresh coals added from time to time. When

Sheepherder bread

the bread was dark brown, it was done, or when it tested dry when poked with a straw. This bread is also superb when toasted.

Sheepherder Bread—II

This one has been adapted for kitchen use, but it has a tangy and delicious open-range taste just as delectable as those baked out on the high and wild plateaus of the Rockies.

1 ½ cups sourdough starter	2 tbsps. melted shortening
4 cups flour	1 tsp. salt
2 tbsps. sugar	¼ tsp. baking soda

Into a large bowl sift the dry ingredients, and dig a well in the center of the sourdough starter. Blend the dry mix into the starter from the edges with enough flour to knead until smooth and shiny. Place in greased pan and let rise. Then shape into two loaves and place in greased bread pan. Bake at 375° until done.

Sourdough Pumpernickel

This is a specialty in some of the backwater communities where the descendants of other early emigrants still live. It is a hard one to make, but well worth the effort. We recommend you don't try this one until you have practiced on other sourdough breads.

1 ½ cups starter	2 cups unsifted rye flour
2 tbsps. chopped caraway seeds	½ cup boiling hot black coffee

Pour boiling coffee over chopped caraway seeds. Let mixture cool and then add it to the flour and starter which have previously been mixed well. Let stand for

Pumpernickel

4 to 8 hours in a warm place, preferably overnight. Then add:

½ cup molasses	3 tbsps. melted shortening
¼ cup powdered skim milk	½ cup whole milk
2 tsps. salt	2¾ cups white flour

1 pkg. active dry yeast

Set in covered bowl until it rises double. Then knead on floured board, and shape into two round loaves on a baking sheet. Let rise until double again, and bake at 350° for half an hour or more, or until done.

You'll find this homemade pumpernickel totally unlike anything you can buy at a store, and it will probably hook you for life. Don't use it for ordinary table bread. Save it for parties, for snacks and lunches. It goes best with cheeses, sausages, salami, and other delights, including cold dark beer in frosted mugs.

Sourdough Raisin Bread

Old Harv, up in Juneau, used to prepare something special for Sundays and holidays—that is, when he felt like it. Naturally it originated in that old slimy sourdough pot, and usually it was something like hot raisin bread, which, spread with peanut butter, sure did hit the spot on lazy days around the fire when the cold rain was soaking down outside on Gastineau Channel.

You make this simply by impregnating with raisins (do it the night before) the sourdough starter you plan to use in your regular sourdough bread recipe. Be sure to use a bigger bowl than usual to hold the working starter, because the raisins make it rise more. Then go ahead and make your bread using the starter with the raisins. You can also make raisin bread rolls and

Sourdough pumpernickel—mouthwatering!

raisin hotcakes the same way—by first filling the starter you're using with raisins and setting overnight.

North Dakota Farmer Bread

As a lad growing up on the lonely prairies of North Dakota, like most kids, I never knew what was good for me. During one rebellious period, I even preferred store-bought bread to my mother's good old home-baked version. "Dark bread," I simply wouldn't touch at all during another painful period. When you're a kid, I guess it's natural to reject what you're told is "good for you," and reach out for new and strange things to try. Matter of fact, I guess this is how one learns what's right and wrong in this world—not from any amount of preachin' or larnin' a kid gets from his older and wiser elders. Don't ask me why.

Anyway, there were a lot of good, real, fine and wholesome things about growing up in rural North Dakota, and many esoteric as well as real solid advantages. Today, at my age I would even call it a privilege.

But you couldn't tell me that when I was straining my bonds, waiting for the ceremonies and festivities and politicians' speeches to end, so I could grab my high school diploma and cut out for other parts of the world on my own. It wasn't until 25 or 30 years later, bloodied and battered by this "outside world," that I returned for a high school reunion and suddenly found myself almost reincarnated, a wiser, more thoughtful, and more appreciative person for the heritage I had run away from so restlessly.

But, no more of that nonsense. Let's get on with the main business here. One of those real, genuine wholesome delights of my youth was good old dark bread, which I once turned up my nose at:

1 cup starter	2 cups warm water
1 pkg. active dry yeast	½ cup brown sugar
1 cup powdered skim milk	2 tsps. salt
6 cups stone-ground wheat flour	2½ tbsps. cooking oil
	¼ cup molasses

Dissolve yeast in warm water, stirring in powdered milk and other ingredients *except* flour. Stir in sourdough starter. Make sure it is a lively starter, otherwise add more yeast. Blend mixture in large bowl that has been warmed. Gradually add the flour, until mixture is turned into dough, then put out on floured board and knead 100 times. Place in greased bowl and cover. When it has doubled in size, divide into two loaves and place in greased bread tins. Cover and let rise again. Glaze tops of loaves with melted cinnamon butter or cooking oil. Bake at 400° for a few minutes, then reduce heat to 375° and bake until done, about a half hour to 45 minutes. Remove from pan and cool on racks.

You'll find this dark bread unlike the bakery product. It is not as coarse, and holds its moisture better. And besides that the kitchen is filled with that tangy nutty flavor of genuine sourdough.

Mouse River Homestead Bread

Here's a loaf the nester gals used to make to trap the farm boys who fell for it like flies buzzing around a hive of wild clover honey. Of course this was before my time, but this is what my older brothers used to tell me, among other things I probably shouldn't have known.

2 cups sourdough starter	1 tsp. baking soda
2 tbsps. melted butter or	3½ cups whole wheat, rye,
margarine	or white flour
½ cup milk	2 tsps. salt
1 tbsp. sugar or honey	

Melt butter or margarine in a saucepan. Add milk and sugar or honey. Turn into mixing bowl. Add starter, stirring in flour, salt, and baking soda. Turn out onto a floured board and knead lightly until smooth and shiny. Let rise until double, or put in warm oven with pan of water for faster rise time. Punch down, and divide into loaves. Let the two loaves rise again until double. Bake in moderate oven, 350°, for about an hour or until loaf pulls away from pan or sounds hollow when tapped lightly.

Prince of Peace Coffee House Bread

While this book was in preparation, a letter arrived from a reader at the Christian Prince of Peace Coffee House in the "long-hair section" of Portland, Oregon.

"Dear Mr. Holm: It is nearly midnight and I just took my sourdough bread out of the oven. I made the No. 1 starter of flour and water on Friday last week and decided to experiment with it today. I had fantastic luck as I have never used sourdough before. My husband and I have been working with the Prince of Peace Coffee House for a year and because we have become interested in Long Hair People and their feelings about natural foods, etc., I have been baking nearly all the bread the family eats. I have wanted to try sourdough and not use any yeast at all in case I needed to bake when yeast wasn't available. Your column did not have a regular bread recipe, so I experimented. I

A melange of sourdough goodies

used 1 cup starter, 4 cups warm water, 1½ teaspoons salt, ½ cup honey, and about 6 cups flour.

I put this in a warm place for awhile, but after an hour I decided to help it along and added 2 cups flour and 1 teaspoon instant yeast. This took 5 hours to rise. I then added 4 cups flour and ½ teaspoon soda and kneaded well, then put back to rise. We went out for dinner and about 3 hours later, I came home to find it running all over the place. I divided it into 3 parts and rolled like a bedroll into loaves. I let this rise about 2 hours, but it could have gone a little longer. It looked and smelled just great. Thank you for helping me discover this 'lost art.' "

Cowpuncher Sourdough Bread

Cowboy cooks, especially those chuckwagon commandos on the spring and fall roundups, were called by many names, including *cocinero*, coosie, cookie, bean master, belly cheater, biscuit roller, dough belly, dough puncher, dough wrangler, grease belly, grub worm, gut robber, pot rustler, Old Woman, and many more unprintable versions.

But one thing about them, they were loyal hands who could throw together rib-stickin' meals under the worst kind of field conditions, and always have it ready when the hands came in tired and saddle sore.

And since cowboys like sourdough bread better than 'most anything, the Camp Robber who could whip up some under field conditions was likely to reign as King of the Roost.

Here's the usual way it was done:

He filled a large pan about two-thirds full of flour, dug a hollow in the center, and poured in some sourdough starter—the amount by guess, by God, and by experience. He then added a teaspoon of soda which had been dissolved in warm water, a small amount of salt, lard or bacon grease, and maybe a bit of sugar or molasses.

Stirring, he worked the dry flour in from the sides, being careful that the soda and shortening were well-mixed. As soon as he had a stiff dough, he floured the fold-down table on the chuckwagon and kneaded the dough on it until thoroughly mixed and shiny.

Meanwhile he had a hot bed of coals readying. Making the dough into loaves, he placed them in the Dutch oven which had been greased with melted lard or bacon, and set alongside the fire to keep warm while the bread was rising. When it had risen, he punched down and let rise again. Finally he placed the hot lid on the oven, set the oven on the fire, raked hot coals onto the lid, and baked until done.

The same method was used for making cowboy "sourdoughs"—hot biscuits, which will be described in the biscuit section.

Bran Date Bread

If the kids don't like oatmeal, but go for All Bran, here's a date bread that will slow them down temporarily.

1¼ cups sifted flour	1 cup pitted dates, cut fine
1½ tsps. baking powder	1 cup All Bran
1 tsp. salt	1 tsp. grated lemon peel
½ cup sourdough starter	2 eggs, beaten
¾ cup buttermilk	¼ cup vegetable oil
¾ cup brown sugar, firmly packed	

Sift dry ingredients together. Dust dates with 1 tablespoon flour mixture, then add the brown sugar, All Bran, and grated lemon peel. Combine ¾ cup buttermilk, 2 beaten eggs, ¼ cup vegetable oil. Add all at once to flour mixture with the sourdough starter, stirring until well-moistened. Pour into greased or wax paper-lined loaf pan about 9x5 inch size. Bake at 350° for one hour. Allow to stand 10 minutes. Remove from pan and cool. Wrap in foil or plastic wrap and place in refrigerator. Spread with butter or cream cheese, or any other spread. It can also be toasted.

Sourdough Banana Bread

Mrs. George Stankey of Missoula, Montana, wrote for some of my columns and enclosed a recipe for Sourdough Banana Bread she had obtained from a University of Montana gal, and it's a good one. We made a couple of improvements in experimenting, however.

⅓ cup shortening	2 cups all-purpose flour
1 cup sugar	1 tsp. salt
1 egg	1 tsp. baking powder
1 cup mashed bananas	½ tsp. baking soda
1 cup sourdough starter	¾ cup chopped walnuts
1 tsp. vanilla, or 1 tsp. grated orange rind	

Cream together the shortening and sugar, add egg, and mix until blended. Stir in bananas and sourdough starter. Add orange rind or vanilla. Sift flour, measure again with salt, baking powder, and soda. Add flour mixture and walnuts to the first mixture, stirring just until blended. Pour into greased 9x5 inch loaf pan. Bake in moderate or 350° oven for 1 hour or until toothpick comes out clean. Cool before slicing.

Myrtle's Original
Chocolate Applesauce Nutbread

This one happened back on the North Dakota prairies one wintry day when the boys and gals gathered at one of the farm homes of a Saturday afternoon. When the hostess was caught short of good old-fashioned sweet things, this is what she came up with—and it's been the cause of a lot of whispered sweet things ever since.

Melt 2 squares unsweetened chocolate (or use two envelopes of "no-melt" chocolate). Cream together ¼ cup shortening, 1 cup sugar, 1 egg and 1 teaspoon vanilla. Mix in ½ cup applesauce and ½ cup sourdough starter. Sift together 2 cups flour, 1 teaspoon baking soda, ½ teaspoon salt. Add to creamed mixture, mixing thoroughly. Blend in the melted chocolate and ½ cup chopped walnuts.

Put batter in greased or wax paper-lined 9x5 inch loaf pan and bake for 55 minutes at 350° (or until done), remove and cool for 10 minutes. Take out of pan and place on rack. When cold, slice thin and spread with butter, margarine, or cream cheese.

Sourdough Applesauce Tea Loaf

Here's another of Myrtle's creations which is at home at an afternoon teen party or a ladies' aid tea.

Cream together ⅓ cup shortening and 1 cup sugar, add 1 egg and 1 teaspoon vanilla, mixing well. Stir in ⅔ cup applesauce and ½ cup sourdough starter.

Sift together 2 cups flour, 1 teaspoon baking soda, ½ teaspoon salt, ¼ teaspoon cinnamon and ¼ teaspoon allspice. Add to creamed mixture, mixing well, and then stir in ½ cup finely chopped walnuts. Place in greased and lined 9x5 inch loaf pan, bake 50 minutes at 350°. Cool about 10 minutes, then remove from pan and place on rack. When cold, slice and spread as desired.

Original Sourdough Tea Loaf

This one can be varied to use chocolate or prunes, or both, with equally tasty effect. It is designed to be sliced thin and spread with butter or cream cheese. It can be stored indefinitely in foil in the freezer.

Cream together 1 cup sugar and ¼ cup shortening. Beat in 1 egg and 1 teaspoon vanilla. Stir in 2 squares melted chocolate and ½ cup starter.

Sift together 2 cups flour, 1 teaspoon soda, ½ teaspoon baking powder, ½ teaspoon salt. Add that to creamed mixture, alternately with 1 cup snipped or cut cooked prunes in juice; stir in ½ cup chopped walnuts. Bake in 9x5 inch loaf pan 1 hour at 350°. Cool for 10 minutes. Remove from pan. Finish cooling on rack.

Applesauce tea loaf

V

BANNOCK BILL THE BISCUIT BAKER

You took the measure of a man in the North Country by the way he threw together a batch of bannock or trail biscuits. This was how old Bannock Bill got his monicker up in the Cariboo region around Mile Post X, according to Harv Smith, who used to bang my ear for hours about his adventures as a trapper and miner.

Bannock on the trail was not only the staff of life, but often its salvation. On the trail you often measured the mileage you made, not in gallons per hour, but in bannocks per horsepower—in this case, shank's-mare. You couldn't take the sourdough starter with you, of course, unless you took along a bag of flour, and you had to go light in order to pack the traps and other gear. It wasn't practical to leave a batch going in the line camps, so you resorted to trail biscuits made this way:

Mix 1 cup flour, 1 teaspoon baking soda, 1 tablespoon dried milk, 2 tablespoons lard or cooking oil or bacon drippings, ½ teaspoon salt. This was generally pre-mixed before you left the cabin.

When you stopped for a meal or to make camp, you added enough water to your mix to make a soft dough. You then greased a frying pan, pre-heated it, propped it up so it caught the reflected heat of the coals, broke off egg-size lumps of dough, rolled them in the grease, and packed them in the pan.

They should be cooked slowly, with care not to let them get too hot or they will burn. The trick is to get them a golden brown on the outside and well-cooked on the inside. It takes practice, but it's an art worth learning.

Many hombres preferred sweet bannock, which was made by adding raisins and sugar to the dough mix for more nourishment on the trail.

When old Bannock Bill was finally back at the base camp and found himself snowed in under a heavy blanket that piled up against the door and windows, he was likely to just get cozy, bake a batch of sourdoughs, and curl up with an old dog-eared copy of *National Geographic* magazine, there not being a *Playboy* in those days.

Bill's Sourdoughs

Mix 2 cups starter with ½ cup flour into which has been blended 1 teaspoon baking soda, 1 teaspoon salt, and 1 tablespoon of melted butter, bacon fat, or cooking oil.

Add more flour if it is too thin, making a stiff dough. Lightly knead to form biscuits and drop in buttered pans. Allow to rise double, brush with melted butter, and bake at about 400° for a few minutes, then reduce heat and cook until done, about 45 minutes. You can also make bread this way, forming loaves instead of biscuits.

Cowboy Sourdoughs

Refer to the chapter "By Bread Alone" and make a sourdough bread dough in the way of the chuckwagon cooks. Then, instead of making it up into loaves, figure on biscuits. Cookie meanwhile would have had a hot bed of coals. Letting dough stand a moment, he would pick up the *gouche* hook and rake a place for the Dutch oven, greasing it generously. The lid was also set on the coals to pre-heat.

Then he would pinch off egg-size pieces of dough, palm them into balls, and roll them in the melted grease as he put them in the oven, to prevent their sticking together. As he filled the oven with the doughballs he jammed them tightly together so they would rise higher and lighter. When the oven was full he placed it off the fire for about 30 minutes to allow the biscuits to rise, while turning his attention to the rest of the meal. At the right time, when the rest of the meal was done, he placed the oven on the coals, covered it with the lid and baked about 10 minutes, serving the "sourdoughs" finger-burnin' hot.

The biscuits are best when hot coals are piled higher on top of the lid, than under the oven. With the heat above, a delicious brown crust forms on top but the center is soft and tender.

It is permissible to peek under the lid during the 10-minute period to see how they are coming along.

The sourdoughs were also called *dough gods, hot rocks, sinkers, sourdough bullets*—but all with deep affection that the cowboys usually tried to hide.

Back at the ranch, when raisins were added to the dough, the biscuits were also called hunkydummy, especially if they were made with baking powder.

It goes without saying that there were as many ways of making sourdough biscuits as there were cooks and camp robbers. So here are a couple of variations:

Sourdough Biscuits—I
This one is also made for the camp Dutch oven. Dig

Sourdough biscuits

a hole in the flour sack and put in a couple of cups of sourdough starter. Sprinkle ½ teaspoon baking soda and ½ teaspoon baking powder, ½ teaspoon salt, and 1 teaspoon sugar over the starter and mix dough by pulling in the flour from around the edges, blending thoroughly. When you have a soft dough, remove immediately. Into a pre-heated Dutch oven, which has melted shortening, lard, or cooking oil in an amount to cover the bottom, drop egg-size pieces of dough and turn until each is well coated with grease.

Place the Dutch oven on a bed of hot coals and put hot coals on the rim of the lid. Don't use too much heat, and inspect frequently after five minutes. These take about 10 minutes to bake.

Sourdough Biscuits—II

This one is a milk-type sourdough starter biscuit. It is worthwhile to keep a milk-type starter going just for these. They are good even when cold, and the dough can also be used for cinnamon rolls. Use cooking oil or bacon fat for shortening. The bacon grease adds a flavor, but the oil is easier to use. Note that a yeast is also used, in addition to baking powder and starter.

Mix together ½ cup starter, 1 cup milk, and 1 cup unsifted flour and let stand in a warm place for 4 to 8 hours. Then add:

1 cup unsifted flour	1 tsp. baking powder
¾ tsp. salt	½ tsp. baking soda
1 tbsp. sugar	½ pkg. active dry yeast

Mix together and turn out onto floured board. Knead lightly 8 to 10 times. Roll out dough to about ¾-inch thickness. Cut into biscuits and dip each in salad oil or warm bacon grease. Place in pan. Cover and let rise about 30 minutes. Bake in a 375° oven for 30 minutes.

One reader, a ranch lady who wrote in about a biscuit recipe that appeared in one of my columns, gave me her method in sixteen words:

"1 cup flour, 1 cup warm fresh milk. Set sponge in the morning, biscuits at night."

In the mail one day came a suspicious-looking package. Once it was determined to be harmless, I opened it and found what looked like several samples of moon rocks brought back by Apollo II. I also found a note with them. It read:

"Dear Mr. Holm—I am sorry I called you a rat fink for putting me on the spot with your sourdough starter recipe. Now please give me the recipe for biscuits. Signed—Sixth Wife."

I recalled some months back the same person had written explaining that her husband had seen my recipe for sourdough starter and demanded she get off the dime. She had signed that letter, "Fifth Wife."

It must be freely admitted that first attempts at sourdough biscuits can easily result in moon rocks, but at the same time a little persistence and practice will produce the real thing eventually. For the benefit of the Court of Domestic Relations, however, I sent Sixth Wife a simplified recipe for biscuits that have all the delicate taste and flavor of old-fashioned sourdough biscuits, with none of the fuss, bother, or skill required. This was developed by my bride, especially for beginners:

Honeymoon Sourdoughs

Mix in a large bowl 1 cup of active starter, 1¼ cups prepared biscuit mix, ½ teaspoon baking powder, and 1 tablespoon cooking oil.

After mixing thoroughly, turn out onto a floured board, knead, and then roll out gently and cut into biscuits. Brush lightly with melted butter or margarine. Bake on a Teflon or greased cookie sheet about 15 minutes at 450°. This makes about 9 large biscuits that, served with honey and butter, will consummate any ceremony.

Miner's Sourdoughs

In the rough-and-ready mine camps of the West and North, a prospector with gold glittering in his eyes and faced with the annoying necessity for "batchin' " all by himself, could make an ersatz biscuit that could pass for the real thing in a pinch. And if actually used with sourdough starter, it turned out to be a real bonanza.

Mix a tablespoon of vinegar in canned cow to the amount of milk called for in one of the simple biscuit recipes. Decrease the amount of baking powder a mite, then go on with the recipe in the usual way.

At first this was used as a sourmilk biscuit in lieu of a starter, but when starter was added to it also by some anonymous experimenter, the results were amazing.

Any leftover biscuits, rather than being thrown away, can be used in many ways. Besides as bases for creamed chipped beef, they can be split, spread with butter, and toasted under the broiler. You can spread them with cheese, salad seasoning, and garlic, or—before baking—roll 'em out round for your favorite pizza shell.

An "expedition" mix can be prepared for use on the trail or on a camping trip, in which all the dry ingredients are prepared in advance at home and packed in plastic bags. All they need is a little liquid, and a carbonated beverage makes a mighty handy "raiser." A sourdough sponge can also be carried right in a bag of flour, just like the old prospectors and trappers did it, then remove and warm up, mix with fresh water in camp, and you have a fresh yeast factory working for you.

Reminder: we recommend you put nothing in a starter except flour and water and possibly dry yeast. Not even salt and sugar.

Cora Stevenson is sort of a landmark in Fossil, Oregon, in spite of the fact that she's less than five feet tall and weighs about 90 pounds soaking wet. She lives alone in this remote eastern Oregon village, tending her garden and chickens. Neighbor folks say she's the only one they know who can weed without stooping, she's built so close to the ground.

In the fall during hunting season, she watches as the dudes come and go after elk, deer, chukars, and quail. She even keeps count of the pickups and campers. She doesn't let on, however, that "her" deer come into her garden each night, leaping the fence easily, and dine upon her carrot tops and the neighbor's raspberry bushes. Most folks in Fossil don't have Aunt Cora's patience—last fall someone got "her" deer on the courthouse lawn. I personally have seen the critters wandering down the single main street at night under the mercury vapor lamp.

Aunt Cora grew up on sourdough, and she's helping a lot of other folks grow up on it, too. She makes her starter thick, almost like biscuit dough. She puts the flour into a wooden bowl, by-guess-and-by-gosh. Then she scoops a well in the flour and into it goes a gob of starter. Into the hollow, she puts the other ingredients

—melted shortening, soda, salt, sugar. With her tiny hands she goes to work on this, picking up the flour, working it into the dough a little at a time, and the doughball seems to rise right before your eyes.

Then on a lightly floured board she begins kneading, adding a little flour from time to time. When it squeaks like bread dough, she rolls it out and cuts it, and places the pan of biscuits over a kettle of boiling water for half an hour uncovered to let the biscuits rise. Then into the oven the pan goes for 20 minutes more, and so to the table and hungry mouths, the biscuits light and delicately browned, and with that heavenly sourdough smell.

"She got her instructions in sourdough making," said Cora's niece by marriage, Mrs. Willard Bowles of Oregon City, "long before the turn of the century when she went to work in a boarding house in Condon. 'Uncle George' Stevenson, whom she married, was an early day Central Oregon teamster, driving the big rigs that hauled the grain from the wheat fields of Condon to Arlington on the Columbia River. Uncle George lived almost entirely on Aunt Cora's sourdough hotbreads for more than 50 years until he died at the untimely age of 88."

Here are some of Aunt Cora's recipes, as passed along by Betty Bowles:

Aunt Cora's Flapjacks

1 egg, beaten	½ tsp. baking soda
½ cup sweet milk	1 tsp. baking powder
1 cup sourdough starter	¾ tsp. salt
¾ cup sifted flour (scant)	2 tsps. sugar

Beat egg, add milk and starter. Sift flour and dry

ingredients. Combine the two mixes. Bake on greased griddle. *However*, don't combine the two mixes until everything else is ready to serve. These hotcakes rise quickly and the batter falls if kept waiting.

Aunt Cora's Biscuits

1½ cups sifted flour	2 tbsps. sugar
3 tsps. baking powder	¼ cup shortening, melted
1 tsp. salt	1½ cups sourdough starter
1½ tsps. baking soda (more if starter is very sour)	

Place flour in bowl, add starter in a well, then add melted shortening and the dry ingredients. Turn out onto a lightly floured board and knead until consistency of bread dough, or of a satiny finish. Pat or roll out dough to ½-inch thickness, cut, and put on a greased pan, coat all sides. Let rise over boiling water for ½ hour. Bake at 425° for 15 to 20 minutes.

Miss Mary Rogers of Mexico, Missouri, also is noted for her sourdough biscuits, made like this:

½ cup starter	1 tbsp. sugar
1 cup milk	¾ tsp. salt
2½ cups flour	2 tsps. baking powder
⅓ cup shortening	½ tsp. baking soda
(lard preferred)	¼ tsp. cream of tartar

At bedtime make a batter of the half-cup of starter, cup of milk, and 1 cup of the flour. Let set overnight if biscuits are wanted for breakfast. If wanted for noon, the batter may be mixed early in the morning and set in a warm place to rise. However, unless the weather is real warm, it is always all right to let it ferment overnight. It will get very light and bubbly.

When ready to mix the biscuits, sift together the re-

maining cup and a half of flour and all other dry ingredients, except the baking soda. Work in shortening
with fingers or a fork. Add the sponge, to which the
soda, dissolved in a little warm water, has been added.
Mix to a soft dough. Knead lightly a few times to get
in shape. Roll out to about ½-inch thickness or a little
more, and cut with a biscuit cutter. Place close together in a well-greased 9x13 inch pan, turning to
grease tops. Cover and set in a warm place to rise for
about 45 minutes. Bake in a 375° oven for 30 to 35
minutes. Leftovers are good split and toasted in sand-
wich toaster.

VI

SWEET-TOOTH TILLY AND SOURDOUGH SAM

THE LEGEND persists in the backwater parts of the North Pacific that doughnuts were invented by thrifty Down East ship captains. To explain this you must start with the hole, around which all doughnut lore centers.

As the legend goes, a stingy New England captain, leaving on a long voyage to the whaling grounds of the Bering Sea, loaded aboard his ship several barrels of small round "cakes" baked by his wife. As a treat for the men on the long expedition, she inserted a walnut or almond in the center. The little cakes were an immediate hit with the sailors, but all those expensive nuts bothered the captain. He figured out a way to avoid a mutiny and save money at the same time. On his next trip he eliminated the nuts, leaving only the hole.

It seems more logical, however, that doughnuts were invented by the whalers themselves. If you have read *Moby Dick* you know how the whales were "tried out" in the try pots on deck after capture and cutting up or flensing, to refine the sperm and whale oil which was used for everything from lubricating delicate instruments and watches to making candles and cooking oils. During the trying out the men worked around the clock, snatching a biscuit or piece of salt pork on the run. Then someone accidentally dropped a biscuit into a hot pot of sperm oil, and in an instant it became a deep-fried cake not unlike our present doughnut. From a deep-fried ship's biscuit to sourdough doughnut batter is only about the length of a harpoon tip.

Anyway, these tales make such good telling that I'm not even going to question them, much less document them. As a footnote, however, I might add that those grease-sodden cakes most Americans have been exposed to in sidewalk doughnut joints for years have earned the sobriquet "sinker." Most of them are so tasteless and doughy that they have to be dunked in hot coffee in order to choke them down your gullet.

But, don't give up hope. Next to the invention of sourdough itself, the greatest American culinary achievement has to be the sourdough doughnuts.

Sourdough Sams

Not even my North Dakota farm gal bride would believe that doughnuts could be made so light and greaseless they almost float on air, until she tried the recipe that I "invented" myself one cold winter day snug in the family room by the fireplace. Don't ask me how the inspiration came to me. It's so simple that it defies explanation. All I know is that everyone who has ever made my sourdough doughnuts has raved about them.

They are not only light, with a distinctive nutty flavor, but they are virtually greaseless. When my bride makes them, in fact, she has just as much cooking oil left as when she started. Moreover the oil is just as clean as it was before she fried the cakes in it.

She now makes a large batch at a time, and those we can keep from eating right away, she freezes for another occasion. Each morning we take from the freezer just enough doughnuts to make up our quota for the day, and let them thaw naturally for half an hour or so before eating. They taste just as fresh as when they came out of the pot.

We also have made the happy discovery that they seem to improve with age, while kept in the freezer. As a matter of fact, this phenomenon applies to most sourdough bakery goods.

Here's how you make 'em. Mix:

½ cup sourdough batter	2 egg yolks or 1 whole egg
½ cup sugar	½ tsp. nutmeg
2 tbsps. shortening	¼ tsp. cinnamon
2 cups flour	½ tsp. baking soda
1 teaspoon baking powder	½ tsp. salt

⅓ cup sour milk or buttermilk

Sift dry ingredients, stir into liquid, roll out, and cut. Then heat some oil to 390° and fry. This is an easy way with no interruptions. Makes 17 doughnuts and holes. Dust with granulated sugar or a mixture of cinnamon and sugar in a shake bag.

A letter from Thelma McCoy of Seaview, Washington, thanked me for some recipes in my column and added a footnote: "Two weeks ago I made sourdough pancakes for breakfast. Our grandson, Brian, had spent the night, so it was special. There was about a cupful of pancake dough left so we added a bit of sugar, spices, and more flour and made 6 of the most delicious doughnuts! Heated just enough shortening or oil in pan the size of *one* doughnut, so it didn't take much and baked them one at a time. Since the sourdough comes from an outdoors man (you) in the sport pages, it was okay for grandson to get into the act! P.S. Always look for your fishing news, too."

Because they are so American, and so good, I think we should call them *Sourdough Sams*.

Myrtle's Applesauce Doughnuts

Here's a superb creation, a sample of which Myrtle sent next door to a neighbor who is a professional baker. He called them the best doughnuts he'd ever tasted.

2⅔ cups flour	½ cup starter
1½ tsps. baking powder	2 tbsps. shortening
½ tsp. baking soda	½ cup sugar
1 tsp. salt	2 egg yolks
½ tsp. nutmeg	½ tsp. vanilla
½ tsp. cinnamon	½ cup applesauce

¼ cup buttermilk (or could substitute 1 tbsp. sour cream for part)

Knead well. Roll out and cut into doughnuts. Let stand. Heat cooking oil to 390°. These take slightly longer to cook. Makes about 2 dozen.

Myrtle says to tell you that for a variation, you can use 1 whole egg instead of 2 egg yolks, and no vanilla. Instead, add ¼ teaspoon of mace.

Sourdough Banana Doughnuts

This one could just as well have been invented by the very same whalers, when they stopped on one of those paradise islands in Micronesia for fresh fruit, water, and cavorting with the native gals. There were plenty of bananas, but taro roots don't make good sourdough batter. Anyway, they probably had their minds on something else. Meanwhile, back in the States, some wholesome farm gal, slavin' over a wood cookstove, thought up this one:

Sift together 2⅔ cups flour, 1½ teaspoons baking powder, ½ teaspoon baking soda, and 1 teaspoon salt.

Applesauce doughnuts

Cream together ½ cup sugar and 3 tablespoons vegetable shortening, add 1 whole egg (or 2 egg yolks) mix well, stir in 1 teaspoon vanilla, ¼ cup buttermilk, ½ cup sourdough starter, and ½ cup mashed ripe bananas (of average size). Add sifted dry ingredients, mix well. Turn dough out onto well-floured board (about half at a time), knead well, adding just enough flour until dough handles well. Roll out, cut into doughnuts, and place on aluminum foil; proceed with remaining dough. Heat cooking oil to 390° and fry. Drain on double layer of paper towels. Sugar if desired. These freeze well. Just place in double plastic bag. To eat, place desired amount on plate at room temperature for about 30 minutes before eating, or warm in oven.

As long as we're talking about all-American goodies, here's another old frontier favorite reported to have been the prize that won over Sweet-Tooth Tilly, a Dawson City filly, who was as fickle as she was desirable. When a fuzzy-cheeked young Klondiker came along one day with the recipe his mom used for cinnamon rolls, Tilly traded her heart and hand for it instead of a diamond-studded ring.

Sourdough Cinnamon Rolls

1 cup starter	2 tbsps. shortening
½ cup dry skim milk	½ cup whole milk
2 tsps. salt	2½ cups flour
3 tbsps. sugar	1½ tsps. baking soda

Mix ingredients together, working in the flour until a good dough results. Divide the dough into two parts, rolling each out into thin cakes, about ¼ inch thick. Do the following with each half: Dot with butter, sprinkle with ¼ to ½ cup of brown sugar mixed with 1

Banana doughnuts

teaspoon of cinnamon. Roll dough into foot-long sizes. Cut off 1-inch slices and place in pan in which has been placed a mixture of 2 tablespoons of melted butter, 1 tablespoon liquid coffee, 2 tablespoons of brown sugar, ½ teaspoon of cinnamon, and a dash of salt.

Let dough rise about an hour and bake at 325°. Serve upside down with sticky mixture on top.

As American as applesauce and Oh-You-Kid is this favorite from the cookshack at many a threshing bee:

Sourdough Applesauce Cake

1 cup starter	1 cup canned or home-made
¼ cup dry skim milk	applesauce
1 cup white flour	

Mix these and let set in covered bowl in a warm place, then:

Cream ½ cup white sugar, ½ cup brown sugar, and ½ cup butter or margarine.

Now add 1 egg, beaten well, and then mix in the following:

½ tsp. salt	½ tsp. allspice
1 tsp. cinnamon	½ tsp. cloves
½ tsp. nutmeg	2 tsps. baking soda

You can also add half a cup of chopped nuts and/or raisins, if desired. Combine all ingredients and beat by hand. Bake at 350° for half to three-quarters of an hour. Test for doneness, and allow to cool in the pan.

Just the smell of this is enough to drive one wild with desire. It is moist and good just like those your mother used to bake on the old wood kitchen range, and no frosting is needed.

For some reason, down through the years, sourdough cooking has taken on the image of being "camp cooking," which is a total injustice to this versatile art. This implies that you can't really come up with more refined culinary delights such as pastries, which is another gross injustice.

One of the most scrumptious treats in my calorie collection is the sourdough prune cake my bride invented herself. Naturally, I call it:

Wild Irish Rose Sourdough Prune Cake

½ cup sourdough starter
½ cup shortening
1½ cups sugar
2 eggs
2 cups sifted flour
1½ tsps. baking soda
1 tsp. cinnamon
½ tsp. salt
1 cup buttermilk
1 cup chopped, drained, cooked prunes
½ cup chopped walnuts

Be sure the starter is warm and very active. Cream the shortening and sugar. Add eggs one at a time, beating well. Add starter and buttermilk—be nice and gentle with the sourdough. Sift and add dry ingredients, prunes, and nuts. Bake at 350° for about 40 minutes in a well-greased and floured cake tin about 9x13 inches in size. Test with finger pressing method. If it springs back, it's ready. This batch will also make 2½ dozen cupcakes, but bake them only 25 minutes. If desired, top with an icing of your choice. Myrtle uses orange cream cheese icing* on this one.

You will be delighted at the smoothness of this batter, as the starter begins working, to say nothing of the praise you'll find heaped upon you for thinking of it in the first place.

---

*See Appendix.

Most of the Forty-niners and Klondikers who made sourdough cooking famous were lean and hungry gents, not given to much palaver or foofooraw when it came to victuals. The work was hard, the hours long, and the rations short—and there was always that pot o' gold at the end of the trail.

For most of them, it was merely a pot of sourdough starter, and if the truth were known, that's what kept them goin'.

Once in a while, however, they'd come upon a prospector who was content and chubby instead of lean and hungry. They knew right off that either he'd just got back from the fleshpots on the Outside, or he'd been livin' off the epitome of all sourdough pastries—chocolate cake.

And if you've got a lean and hungry hombre around your house, try out my bride's recipe and he'll wind up docile and contented—like me.

Myrtle's Sourdough Chocolate Cake

Mix ½ cup sourdough starter with ¼ cup non-fat dry milk, 1½ cups flour, and 1 cup water. Mix well and let stand a couple hours in a warm place, until that delectable yeasty smell comes to you like an elixir of the gods.

Cream ½ cup shortening and 1 cup sugar. Add 1 teaspoon vanilla, 1 teaspoon red vegetable coloring, ½ teaspoon salt, 1½ teaspoons soda. Add 2 eggs one at a time and mix well. Then add 3 squares melted chocolate. Stir this creamed mixture into the sourdough mix. Gently blend. Pour into a cake tin about 7x11 inch size. Bake at 350° for 35 to 40 minutes.

Myrtle's Burnt Sugar Spice Cake

My bride found this recipe among her old high school scrapbooks. One rainy day recently, without telling me what she was doing, she whipped up a batch. When I came home and spotted a plate of fresh golden brown wedges waiting for my approval, just one look told me she had struck paydirt again. And the first bite confirmed it.

Here's how she did it:
In a large mixing bowl, sift together 2 cups flour, 1 cup sugar, 1 teaspoon baking soda, ½ teaspoon salt, 1 teaspoon cinnamon, ½ teaspoon cloves, ½ teaspoon nutmeg.

Add ½ cup vegetable shortening or butter, ½ cup sour milk or buttermilk, 3 tablespoons burnt sugar syrup (see below), 2 eggs, and ½ cup sourdough starter.

Beat 3 minutes with electric mixer. Fold in ½ cup finely chopped nuts and ½ cup golden seedless raisins. Bake in a greased and floured 13x9½ inch pan for 35 to 40 minutes at 350°.

Burnt Sugar Syrup

Put ½ cup granulated sugar in a small skillet and stir over a medium high heat until melted, and quite dark. Remove from heat, add ¼ cup water, and stir in well, but be careful as the syrup splatters when water is added. (See also Appendix).

Myrtle had no sooner completed this triumph, than she turned around and came up with another—one that had been hidden away in her old scrapbooks and forgotten for years. One bite of these delights will send you soaring back down the nostalgia trail.

Myrtle's Old-Fashioned Spicy Mounds

Mix together ¼ cup soft shortening, ½ cup brown sugar, 1 medium egg, ½ cup molasses, and ½ cup sourdough starter.

To this add 1 teaspoon baking soda dissolved in 1 tablespoon hot water. Sift together 2 cups flour, ½ teaspoon salt, 1 teaspoon ginger, ½ teaspoon nutmeg, ½ teaspoon cloves, and ½ teaspoon cinnamon. Mix well and add to the first batch of ingredients.

Drop onto a Teflon-coated or lightly greased cookie sheet teaspoon-size bites, and bake at 400° about 10 minutes. Makes 54 cookies. When cool, frost with the following:

Creamy Icing

1 cup confectioners sugar	2 tbsps. cream or condensed
¼ tsp. maple flavoring	milk

Blend thoroughly until it can be spread very smooth. (See also Appendix).

After trying the Spicy Mounds, you'll tend to forget that good cookies are really hard to come by, even in polite society. Out on the trail and in the camps they are almost unknown. Don't ask me why this is so, because there really is no mystery about them, nor are they difficult to make—provided you have a good workable recipe, like my secret one for:

Burnt sugar spice cake

Ghost Town Sourdough Cookies

½ cup shortening
1½ cups brown sugar
2 eggs
½ cup buttermilk or sour milk
½ cup sourdough starter
2 cups sifted flour
1 tsp. baking soda
1 tsp. baking powder
1 tsp. salt
1 tsp. cinnamon
½ tsp. allspice
3 cups quick-cooked rolled oats
1 cup raisins
½ cup walnuts

Cream shortening, sugar, and eggs to a light and fluffy mixture. Stir in buttermilk and starter, then stir in sifted dry ingredients, and rolled oats, nuts, and raisins. Drop cookie-sized gobs two inches apart on greased sheet and bake at 375° for 10 minutes. This recipe can be varied by reducing brown sugar and adding equal amounts of honey, and/or molasses. You can also omit the raisins and add 1 cup finely cut dates.

Sourdough Rum Roll

Up in Alaska before the big oil strikes on Cook Inlet and the North Slope, winters were long and there wasn't much excitement in being holed up at outlying camps or in snow-laden cabins. Along about Thanksgiving when it began to snow in earnest, the homesteaders and trappers prepared their holiday fruit cakes. With this one, by Christmas time it was good enough to fill your belly as well as raise your spirits.

1½ cups sourdough starter
4 eggs
4 cups flour
½ cup shortening or oil
1 cup brown sugar
1 cup white sugar
1 tsp. baking soda
2 tsps. salt
1 cup chopped almonds
1½ cups golden raisins
1 cup currants
3 cups candied fruit assortment
1½ tsps. cinnamon
1 tsp. nutmeg
½ tsp. allspice
½ pint rum, brandy, or hard cider

Ghost Town sourdough cookies; chocolate drops; Myrtle's Old-fashioned Spicy Mounds

After washing and preparing the fruit, mix with the booze and set aside in a warm place overnight. Beat the eggs and add them to a creamed mixture of sugar, condiments, spices, and shortening.

Sift the remaining dry ingredients—soda, flour, salt —into the sourdough starter and mix well. Combine all the mixes and spoon into two loaf-size pans heavily greased and lined with wax paper. Put pans on rack in oven set for 275°. Put a shallow pan of warm water under them. Bake for 2½ hours. Remove and cool cakes on racks. When cool, wrap individually in cheesecloth and saturate the cloth with rum or brandy. Package in aluminum foil and place in cooler for two or three weeks before opening.

Chocolate Nut Drops

These were another creation by Myrtle, and when samples were taken to the office, the gals all went on strike until we gave them the "secret" recipe.

2 envelopes "no-melt" chocolate	¼ cup sour milk
½ cup salad oil	¼ cup starter
1½ cups brown sugar, packed	1 tsp. vanilla
1 egg, unbeaten	1 cup chopped nuts
	2 cups sifted flour
	¼ tsp. baking soda
½ tsp. salt	

Sift together the flour, baking soda, and salt. Blend the chocolate, oil, and brown sugar. Add the egg and beat well. Then stir in the vanilla, sour milk, and starter. Add the sifted dry ingredients and mix well. Stir in the chopped nuts. Drop by teaspoon onto Teflon cookie sheet, place in refrigerator. When chilled, bake at 350° for 10 minutes. Keep one filled cookie sheet in refrigerator while the other bakes. This makes about 4 dozen. Cover with:

Chocolate Icing

Melt ½ cup semi-sweet chocolate morsels. Remove from heat, stir in 2 tablespoons hot water. Mix well and add 2 tablespoons soft butter or margarine, 1½ cups sifted confectioner's sugar, a small pinch of salt, and ½ teaspoon vanilla. Beat until smooth. Frost cookies when they are cool. (See also Appendix).

These nut drops are crisp and tasty with that faint tang of sourdough, and they seem to taste even better the longer they stand. They keep nicely in the freezer, too.

Chocolate Honey Drops

Here's another one of Myrtle's home creations that has been a big hit with the kids (including the biggest and oldest). Mix together ¼ cup soft shortening, ½ cup brown sugar (packed), 1 medium-size egg, ½ cup honey, 1 teaspoon vanilla, and ½ cup sourdough starter.

Add 1 teaspoon baking soda dissolved in 1 tablespoon hot water. Sift together 2 cups flour and ½ teaspoon salt and add to the above, mixing well.

Blend in 2 envelopes pre-melted unsweetened chocolate and ½ cup chopped walnuts, if desired. Drop by teaspoon onto Teflon-coated or lightly greased cookie sheet. Bake at 400° about 9 minutes. These do not spread. Watch closely and remove from oven promptly.

Top with chocolate icing or creamy white icing and decorate each with a milk-chocolate morsel.

VII

CHUCKWAGON CHUCKLES

MOST OF THE old Sourdoughs in the mining camps, and the chuckwagon pot-bangers on the cattle range, wouldn't have been caught dead making muffins. A mite too sissified for the likes o' them, they'd mutter.

This is one sourdough trick that the ladies came up with, long after the frontier had been tamed—but by then the old-timers didn't know what they were missing anyhow.

One little lady, who happens to be a favorite of mine, concocted this one. Try it and you'll know why I voted for the institution of matrimony.

Dakota Prairie Muffins

1 cup whole bran	½ tsp. baking soda
1½ cups flour	⅓ cup sugar
1 cup buttermilk	½ tsp. salt
¼ cup shortening	1 egg
1½ tsp. baking powder	½ cup sourdough starter

Sift together the flour, baking powder and soda, and salt. To soften the bran, soak in buttermilk. Cream the shortening and sugar, and beat in the egg. Stir in the bran mixture and starter, then fold in dry ingredients until just moist. Add ½ cup raisins if desired. Drop in greased muffin pans. Bake at 375° for 35 minutes. Makes 8 muffins.

Note: With all sourdough recipes, slightly longer baking time is required than normal—sometimes 10 minutes longer. For this reason, testing is recommended in all recipes.

Sourdough Muffins

1½ cups white flour	1 egg
½ cup whole wheat flour	1 cup chopped raisins
½ cup shortening, melted	1 tsp. salt
½ cup sugar	1 tsp. baking soda
½ cup canned cow	½ cup starter

Mix ingredients thoroughly and add enough sourdough starter to make the mixture moist, or about half a cup. Stir in carefully, don't over-mix. Bake in greased muffin pans at 350° for about half an hour or until done.

Most folks think of the cattleman's West as one of grizzled frontier ranchers, or refugees from Texas after the Civil War, carving an empire out of the wilderness with nothing but guts and a shoestring. It has long since been forgotten that the cattle industry in the West of the post-Civil War period was financed in large part by European investors, particularly English and German nobility. Moreover, many of these foreign owners came across the Big Pond and traveled out to the frontier to look over their empires in person. Many stayed just long enough to go on some real whingding hunting safaris, but others stayed and settled down in the West, and their descendants are still found in large numbers throughout the cattle country.

Naturally, an Englishman had to have his muffins— or at least this is the way the story goes—and many a frontier cook tried to master this strange technique.

Actually, however, English muffins are easy to make and nowadays there has been a revival of them in the home kitchens all across the land, and most bakeries now offer them, as well.

English muffins, as you will see, are not baked but more or less "roasted" on a griddle. They are noted for their long-keeping qualities. They can be frozen and kept indefinitely. And all you have to do is take them out of the freezer, thaw and split them, pop them in the toaster, then spread with butter and jam.

This one, developed with the use of good old sourdough starter, was probably the secret ingredient that kept some of those English noblemen out there on the range.

English Sourdough Muffins

1 cup sourdough starter	2 cups warm water (110°)
2 pkgs. active dry yeast	½ cup oil or shortening
½ cup non-fat dry milk	1 tbsp. sugar
6 cups flour	3½ tsps. salt
1 cup cornmeal	

Dissolve yeast in warm water. In a large mixing bowl add to the yeast water, dry milk, sugar, salt, shortening, and 2 cups of the flour. Then blend in the starter. Add the remaining flour to make a stiff dough. Turn out dough onto a floured board. Knead until smooth, about 10 minutes. Place in a greased bowl. Roll over once to coat the dough with grease. Cover and let rise to double size. Punch down, cover and let stand for 10 minutes. Then turn out on floured board and roll out to ½-inch thick. Cut with cutter into 3-inch rounds. Cover these and let raise until light, about 1½ hours. Sprinkle cornmeal on Teflon cookie sheets and place patties on it, well spaced. Sprinkle more cornmeal on top. Let rise until puffy. Then carefully lift off with pancake turner and place upside-down in Dutch oven or electric frying pan that has been pre-heated to 375°. Bake for about 10 minutes or until a golden tan, turning to bake both sides. Let cool on racks. Split them before using, or before freezing.

Sourdough Pizza Shells

Pizza is about as "Western" as the Mona Lisa, but maybe this one comes from the western part of Italy where all those cowboy-and-Indians movies are being made. Anyhow, a lot of folks hereabouts like it, so here's a quick and easy crust to make.

1 cup sourdough starter	1 tsp. salt
1 tbsp. melted shortening	1 cup flour

Mix ingredients, working in the flour until you have a soft dough. Roll out into a flat shape. Dash oil over a dough sheet and place dough on it. Bake about 5 minutes. It doesn't take long, so watch carefully. Have pizza sauce ready to spread with cheese and sausage. Then bake pizza as usual. An Italian friend of mine, by the way, never ceases to shake his head at the way Americans have taken to this. The real pizza, he said, is simply a dessert, and eating it for the main course is like making a meal of apple pie.

Oh, well, I also have some Japanese friends, and they habitually eat their dessert before they start the main meal.

Rocky Mountain Cornbread

If you like cornbread, you'll like this one. In fact, even if you *don't* like cornbread, you'll like this one.

It's an old-fashioned favorite from Mexico to the Arctic.

½ cup sourdough starter	½ cup sour cream or yogurt
2 tbsps. margarine, melted	2 eggs, stirred
½ cup cornmeal	1 cup white flour
½ tsp. salt	½ tsp. cream of tartar
1 tbsp. sugar	½ tsp. baking powder

Mix ingredients in the above order, stirring only enough to blend the mixture. Pour into a buttered pan. Bake in a 375° to 400° oven for about 15 minutes.

Mendenhall Sourdough Gingerbread

I first tasted this dessert in Juneau, at a little hole-in-the-wall cafe on the road to the Mendenhall Glacier. I don't remember the name of the cafe, but I do remember the dessert, and it deserves its majestic name.

1 cup sourdough starter	½ cup brown sugar
½ cup hot water	1 egg
½ cup molasses	1½ cups flour
½ tsp. salt	1 tsp. ginger
1 tsp. baking soda	1 tsp. cinnamon
½ cup shortening	

Cream brown sugar and shortening and beat. Then add molasses and egg, beating continuously. Sift dry ingredients and blend into hot water, then beat into creamy mixture. As the last step, add the sourdough starter slowly, mixing carefully to maintain a bubbly batter. Bake in pan at 375° for about 30 minutes or until done. Serve with whipped cream or ice cream while still hot.

Flathead Potato Bread

One of our favorite parts of the world is the Flat-

Sourdough pizza

head Lake country of northwestern Montana. In the lee of the dark blue Mission Range, there is a certain quality to the sky and the mountains and the water that fills us with peace and tranquil thoughts. And a favorite in this valley is a hidden spot on the east side of the lake, at the head of a little cove called Yellow Bay. Farther up on the lake, there used to be a nondescript rural cafe, run by a flatland furriner, a refugee from the Midwest, who brought this recipe for potato bread west with him. It probably came across on a boat from Europe originally with his forebears. We're glad it did.

5 to 6 new spuds	1 tbsp. salt
2½ cups flour	1 tsp. baking soda
1 pkg. active dry yeast	1 cup sourdough starter

Boil the potatoes and mash them good, saving the water in which they were boiled. Pour this over the mashed potatoes (reserving a small amount), and add another quart of cold water. Stir in the flour. Add package of yeast which has been dissolved in the reserved potato water. Let mixture rise overnight. The next morning, strain the mixture and add a little more flour, stirring it in until you have a stiff batter. Then add 1 teaspoon of baking soda and let rise again. Next add 1 tablespoon of salt and knead some more flour into it. Knead dough 100 times. Mold into four or five loaves, let rise again, then bake at least an hour in a 375° oven.

Dehorn Butterhorns

Down along the waterfront in Seattle, First Avenue in the old days, before the modern city planners began their urban renewal campaigns, was known to every miner, logger, construction hand, and sailor as *Skid-*

Sourdough "little pizzas"

road. It got its name in the early days of Seattle when that part of the city was being logged off and the logs were transported to the water on what is known as a "skidroad" in woods jargon. Later writers, who hadn't been farther out into the woods than the neighborhood park, misunderstood the term as applied to the honkytonk section of Seattle (and other cities on the West Coast) as "Skidrow." This was picked up by anonymous staff writers on the big Eastern magazines, most of whom didn't know a Douglas fir from a pink rhododendron, and given mass circulation. My friend, the late Stewart Holbrook, who came out of the logging camps to become a major contemporary historian, spent most of his later life trying to correct this misnomer.

Anyway, one of my uncles, with the monicker of Black Jack Holm, was a well-known woods boss in the Duluth, Minnesota, region before the logging industry shifted to the Pacific Northwest. One of his expressions was "dehorn," meaning a wretched, broken-down logger, who had gone off the wagon and was reduced to cadging drinks in waterfront bars, or to squeezin' out canned heat through an old sock.

My first impression of Seattle's Skidroad and its old waterfront dives was of dehorns begging for drinks and subsisting on stale butterhorns the barkeep kept under a fly-specked glass cover on the backbar.

For years afterwards I couldn't stand the sight of a butterhorn, until I was treated to one made from this recipe in Fairbanks:

1 cup sourdough starter	2 tbsps. shortening or oil
1 egg, well beaten	¼ tsp. baking powder
1 cup flour	¼ tsp. baking soda
½ tsp. salt	2 tbsps. sugar
½ pkg. dry yeast	extra flour (½ cup)

Mix dry ingredients, except extra flour. Blend in sourdough starter carefully as the last step. Flour a board with a layer of extra flour, place mixture on it. and knead thoroughly and vigorously until smooth. Let rise in greased bowl until doubled. Roll out on floured board. Paint with melted butter and sprinkle with a mixture of cinnamon and sugar. Roll up and slice off pieces about half an inch thick. Place pieces on greased cookie sheet, flattening each one. Let rise until fluffy. Bake at 375°, about 15 to 20 minutes. Spread while hot with an icing made of confectioner's sugar, butter, vanilla, and hot water. Sprinkle with chopped almonds or walnuts, or eat plain.

My bride's parents, Tom and Annie Tate, came over from County Down in the middle of the last century, and helped settle the wild prairies on the border between North Dakota and Saskatchewan. One of Myrtle's earliest memories is of hot Irish soda bread.

Irish Soda Bread

4 cups sifted white flour	2 tsps. baking soda
1 tsp. salt	1 cup buttermilk or
1 tsp. sugar	sour milk

Sift the dry ingredients several times through your fingers. Add milk gradually, stirring well. Turn the dough out onto a floured board and knead lightly and briefly. Shape into a round flat loaf and cut a deep

cross from side to side. Bake in a flat pan in a 450°
oven for 45 minutes.

Serve hot with butter, jam, or honey. Raisins or
currants could also be added to the dough, but the old-
time bread did not use these. Leftover bread can be
used in corned beef and cabbage or Irish stews. Or,
next morning, brown the leftover bread with a little
bacon fat and serve for breakfast with a fried egg on
top and bacon on the side.

Oatmeal Bannocks

Contrary to pulp fiction writers, bannock is not a
frontier word, but an old Gaelic word for tea biscuits
or big round cakes that have been cut into pie-shaped
wedges for serving.

Oatmeal bannock is made from yeast dough and en-
riched with uncooked oatmeal and currants.

2½ cups unsifted flour	½ cup milk
⅓ cup sugar	½ cup water
¾ tsp. salt	¼ cup or ½ stick
1 cup uncooked old-	margarine
fashioned rolled oats	1 egg
2 pkgs. active dry yeast	1 cup currants

Thoroughly mix about a third of the flour with the
sugar, salt, rolled oats, and undissolved yeast in a large
bowl. Combine the milk, water, and margarine in a
saucepan. Heat over low fire until warm. Gradually
add liquid to dry ingredients and beat two minutes.
Add egg and ½ cup flour or just enough to make a thick
batter. Beat vigorously for a couple of minutes. Stir
in enough additional flour to make a soft dough. Turn
out onto floured board and knead until smooth and
elastic. Place in greased bowl, turning over to grease
all sides. Cover and let rise in a warm place until dou-

bled. Then punch dough down, turn out onto floured board, and knead in currants.

Divide in half and roll each into an 8-inch circle. Place them in greased 8-inch round cake pans. Cut each into wedges with a sharp knife, but not all the way through to the pan. Cover and let rise until double again. Then bake in a 375° oven for 20 minutes or until done. Remove and cool. Freeze for later use what is not immediately needed.

It may seem incongruous that in this age, with a supermarket at every intersection and vehicles that will go anywhere, there should be a need or such a demand for so-called "survival" kits designed to save a person who ventures off the pavement, from his own folly.

In the olden days on the frontier you could drop a man down in the wilderness hundreds of miles from the nearest settlement with nothing but a jackknife and he'd show up weeks later looking as if he'd taken a sojourn at a vacation resort.

Living off the land was part of his upbringing, and he thought so little about it that few journals or letters of those days even mention it.

In this age of freeze-dried food, powdered milk and eggs, vitamin tablets, and other concentrated energy packages, this concept of emergency survival rations has become almost an industry—and a large percentage of it is based on the uneasiness modern man has about his own ability to cope with his natural environment once he is out of sight of a freeway. How much of it is hokum and how much simple nostalgic longing —like the Madison Avenue adventurer who commutes to work in a four-wheel-drive safari vehicle to fulfill some inner urging—no one knows.

Sometimes, of course, a camping or hiking trip turns into a test of survival, not because you plan it that way, but by accident or because of unpredictable weather.

Most of the commercial survival food is expensive as well as bulky and tasteless, as I learned years ago when I flew my own airplane on hunting and fishing trips to Canada, Alaska, and remote places. Eventually I heard about a more practical ration that was just as good and cost practically nothing.

For those hunters, hikers, campers, private pilots, skiers, fishermen, rangers, and others who might want to try it, and not pay the outrageous prices asked for "survival" foods, here is a really superb recipe that you can have fun preparing on dull winter days—although it isn't strictly a "sourdough" type product.

I call them "Oatkins." An average batch makes about 100 survival bars about the size of a piece of caramel. Six of these pieces, along with plenty of water, would keep you going all day. Most survival kits could be replaced, in a pinch, with some fish line, a knife or hatchet, and a pound or two of Oatkins.

Don's Survival Oatkins

Assemble the ingredients: 2 tablespoons of honey, domestic or wild, 3 cups of oatmeal (or bran flakes or wheat germ), 2½ cups powdered skim milk, 1 cup sugar, 3 tablespoons water, 1 package of gelatin dessert in your favorite flavor.

First mix water and honey together and bring to a boil. Then mix in the gelatin. Mix dry ingredients together. Stir in the water-honey-gelatin mixture, blending well in a large bowl. It may be necessary to add more water, but do so a little at a time, and sparingly. The mixture must be moist enough to mold, but not wet, for it has to dehydrate later. You can add raisins or dried fruit, but it won't keep as long.

After mixing, mold the dough into a flat cake tin, about 7x11 inch size. Place in oven set at "warm" and leave the door ajar for several hours or until the dough is thoroughly dry. Don't use more heat than this or the mixture will "cook" and then won't keep. One reader wanted to know if rum added to Oatkins would work. Sure, but the dehydration eliminates the alcohol. I recommended he take his rum separately.

When done, let stand and cool, then cut into bite-size pieces and wrap individually in aluminum foil. The bars will keep indefinitely with refrigeration, for weeks without. A handful of pieces in your pocket or fishing vest will give you enough energy to go all day. The bars can also be boiled with a little fresh water over a campfire for a wholesome hot meal.

They taste like candy, but are also nutritious. You can also take them to the office for a pick-me-up snack. After all, isn't survival the basic drive in most offices these civilized days?

Tip: While you have the warming oven in use, why not make some jerky at the same time? For simple instructions on this ancient and honorable art of preserving beef and red-meated wild game, see *The Old-Fashioned Dutch Oven Cookbook* (The Caxton Printers, Ltd., Caldwell, Idaho).

Finally, as we come reluctantly to the end of the Sourdough Trail, I have before me a long letter from Bert Carey of Bellingham, Washington, who wrote relating some of his personal experiences in the North Country, with sourdough, Dutch ovens, and other frontier miracles.

He ended up with a poem.

"I, myself, contributed the first two verses," he said, "and found the others in an old prospector's cabin in the high Sierras."

Here are a couple of the verses:

Of all the grub that's put out for men to eat,
And that includes apple pie to rare red meat,
The cook who wins the prize is the one who's in the
  know,
And at breakfast, dinner, and supper, feeds them
  sourdough.
He's hunted the hills since daylight for gold—
It's bent his back and made him old,
But he comes in at night, his face all aglow,
A-knowin' he's gonna get beans and sourdough.

Adios, amigos!

APPENDIX

Arbuckle Coffee

FOR FULL ENJOYMENT of sourdough cooking, especially
during the long winter months when sourdough flapjacks taste so good, smothered in maple syrup or blue-
berry preserves, there is nothing to replace good fresh
coffee or ice cold milk.

In the olden days, out on the range, or in the woods,
there was no such thing as fresh milk. If you had any
milk at all it was canned milk or "canned cow," and the
most common were Carnation and Eagle Brand. The
Carnation had a sort of burnt taste to it, which made
it distinctive, and there was a good deal of difference
of opinion as to which brands were the best.

As for the coffee, especially on the cattleman's frontier, there was nothing but Arbuckle's. In those days
of the post-Civil War period, all coffee came in bags
of green beans. It had to be roasted before using, and
most housewives did this in the oven, in the Dutch oven
or an iron skillet. When I was a kid, we could already
buy it roasted from the store, and even have it ground
for us in a big bitter-sweet-smelling grinder turned
by hand.

Arbuckle was the product of two Arbuckle brothers,
wholesale grocers of Pittsburgh, Pennsylvania, who
conceived the idea of shipping coffee already roasted.
They developed a process of coating the roasted beans

with a mixture of sugar and egg white to seal in the fresh flavor.

Arbuckle coffee became so popular in the West that it was a household word. The coffee came in one-pound brightly colored bags with the word *Arbuckle* printed boldly on them, beneath an imprint of a flying angel wearing a long flowing skirt and a streaming red neckerchief around her neck. Beneath this was the legend *Ariosa Coffee*. Inside was a coupon with a facsimile signature of the Arbuckle Brothers, and at one time a red and white candy stick was packed in each sack. The chuckwagon cook used this as bait for volunteers to grind the coffee for the evening meal. He usually had plenty of takers among the sweet-toothed cowboys.

Incidentally, the camp cook usually got the waddies up at the first crack of light with this chant, given to the accompaniment of a spoon banged on an empty pot:

> *Wake up, Jacob!*
> *Day's a-breakin',*
> *Beans in the pot,*
> *An' sourdough's a-bakin'!*

It is possible to buy whole-bean coffee today and grind it yourself. Small inexpensive home coffee grinders are available from a number of sources, without having to haunt the antique bazaars. In most metropolitan areas, you will find coffee distributors and packers who not only have coffee beans, but have them in blender's varieties from all the major coffee growing areas—Kenya, Costa Rica, Brazil, Guatemala, and many others. Some of these coffee packers also have retail stores which sell, packaged for home and gift use, whole beans in each variety and also blends of several

Coffee time

varieties. Many of these retail outlets also sell coffee brewers and coffee mills.

If you like good coffee, it will be well worth your effort to develop the connoisseur's approach and locate your own personal source of beans and blends.

This may sound strange, coming from an hombre who was brought up on camp-style coffee. I still think it is hard to beat coffee made by filling an empty gallon can with cold water, throwing in a couple of handsful of coffee and the egg shells from breakfast, and letting it boil for a couple of hours, or until it floats a spur or a six-gun.

There sure is nothing to beat the aroma of coffee made like this, but in my old age I have developed a stomach sensitive to such acid concoctions, and now prefer my coffee hand-ground of fresh roasted beans in a blend I usually arrive at by mixing a bit of Kenya with some hillside Costa Rican and Guatemalan varieties. No two blends turn out the same, so there is no use trying to detail them.

The key to making this gourmet coffee, even with fresh roasted beans, is in the *water*. It is virtually impossible to find good, potable drinking water anywhere in the world anymore. Most water systems, even where the source is relatively pollution-free, are so heavily spiked with chlorine and other agents as to make them safe but undrinkable. Even the famed Bull Run water supply of the Portland, Oregon, metropolitan area, which originates in a guarded 100-square-mile mountain reserve fed by pure glacial run-off, is today heavily chlorinated.

It is no longer possible to obtain the pure quill that you require for the best coffee, from any municipal water system—and I wouldn't recommend drinking anything that wasn't treated these days.*

I discovered an answer while on a 16-day offshore big game fishing voyage off the mouth of the Sea of Cortez below Cabo San Lucas. The 85-foot sport fisherman I was on had a water-maker which could produce from raw sea water about 20 gallons of pure fresh water per hour when underway. It operated off the heat from the main engine exhausts.

This water was so good, coming out of the refrigerated fountain in the main salon, that I preferred it to anything else aboard, including the liberal stores of chuckle juice. I drank it by the gallon, savoring every drop. The coffee made aboard with this water also was better than anything I'd tasted before, although in the interests of economy the cook used a poor brand of ordinary supermarket vacuum-packed blend.

Recently, a number of firms have offered small home water-makers, some operated by electricity, some by a hotplate or even a camp stove, which can produce a gallon or two of pure water a day out of tap water or even out of polluted water. There should be more market research in this field, and more sophisticated home and camp water-makers developed, but until then these appear to be the only practical ones available.

Even if it makes only a gallon a day, a water-maker will pay for itself in the finest of coffee brew. Once you've tried a fresh roasted blend made with pure filtered water, you'll never be able to stand the ordinary java.

---

*One exception is Enterprise, Oregon, the small cattle and lumbering town in the Wallowa Mountains. The water is so good there, folks prefer it to milk or coffee—if not to harder stuff.

Toppings

Chocolate Frosting: Cream together 2½ cups sifted confectioner's sugar, 2 tablespoons butter or margarine, ¼ teaspoon salt with 3 tablespoons of milk, hot water or coffee. Blend in ⅔ cup semi-sweet chocolate chips, melted and slightly cooled, and ½ teaspoon vanilla. Spread on cake.

Creamy Chocolate Icing: Beat together 3 cups confectioner's sugar, ⅓ cup soft butter or margarine, and ¼ teaspoon salt. Add 1 egg, 1 teaspoon vanilla, and 3 squares unsweetened chocolate, melted. Add 2 to 3 tablespoons milk, gradually beating until smooth. If necessary, chill until ready to spread.

Icing for Burnt Sugar Spice Cake: Mix and beat until smooth, 3 cups sifted confectioner's sugar, ¼ cup soft butter or margarine, ¼ teaspoon salt, 3 tablespoons burnt sugar syrup,* 1 teaspoon vanilla, and about 3 tablespoons of 10% milk or condensed milk to reach spreading consistency.

Prune Icing: Cream ⅓ cup margarine or butter, add 3 tablespoons prune juice and 1 tablespoon lemon juice, 1 teaspoon salt, and 3 cups powdered sugar. Beat until smooth and creamy. Will frost the tops and sides of 2 layers or one 3x9 inch loaf cake.

Maple Icing (for Spicy Mounds): Blend together 1 cup confectioner's sugar, 2 tablespoons top milk (10%), and 3 drops maple flavoring.

Orange Cream Cheese Frosting: Blend a 3-ounce package of cream cheese and 1 tablespoon soft butter or margarine. Add 2 cups confectioner's sugar, mixing well. Then add 1 or 2 tablespoons of orange juice, just enough to make the icing spread nicely.

---

*See page 103.

Maraschino Cherry Icing: Combine a 1-pound package of powdered sugar, 2/3 stick of margarine, and 3 tablespoons maraschino cherry syrup. Beat with electric mixer until creamy and smooth.

Cooking Terms

BAKE: To cook using dry heat, as in an oven.

BATTER: A thick liquid mixture of flour, water, milk, eggs, and other ingredients prepared for baking.

BEAT: To blend ingredients together and whip with a spoon, paddle, electric mixer, or other instrument, in order to combine the ingredients (such as whipping cream or egg whites) with air.

BIND: To hold a mixture together by adding liquid, beaten eggs, or cream.

BOIL: To heat in liquid to a temperature that raises bubbles or boils.

BREAD: To roll in flour or crumbs.

BROWN: To cook quickly at high heat to make a crust, then reduce temperature until done.

CREAM: To beat or stir shortening, butter, or fats until light and fluffy, with or without sugar, flour, and other ingredients.

FOLD: To blend a mixture with liquid by cutting deep with spoon, and turning bottom over on top until fully blended.

DILUTE: Thin by adding liquids.

GLAZE: To coat with a mixture of syrup, gelatin, egg yolks, or cornstarch, also to brown the top coating of bread in the oven.

LEAVEN: To lighten a mixture by adding yeast, baking powder, baking soda, or eggs.

KNEAD: To work dough with hands, using a folding and pressing motion until smooth and spongy.

SCALD: To pour boiling water over dry foods; for liquids, to heat quickly until roiling.

SIFT: To shake dry ingredients, such as sugar, flour, seasonings, and baking powder, together through a sieve or sifter.

THICKEN: To give more body to a mixture by adding flour, cornstarch, cream, or egg.

Baking Temperatures

Slow Oven	=	200° to 275° F.
Moderately Slow	=	300° F.
Moderate	=	325° to 375° F.
Moderately Hot	=	400° F.
Hot	=	425° to 450° F.
Very Hot	=	475° to 525° F.

Measures

Dash	=	2 to 3 drops	=	———
3 tsps.	=	1 tbsp.	=	½ fluid oz.
4 tbsps.	=	¼ cup	=	2 fluid ozs.
8 ″	=	½ ″	=	4 ″ ″
12 ″	=	¾ ″	=	6 ″ ″
16 ″	=	1 ″	=	8 ″ ″
2 cups	=	16 fluid ozs.	=	1 pint
4 ″	=	32 ″ ″	=	1 quart
4 quarts	=	1 gallon	=	———
8 ″	=	1 peck	=	———
4 pecks	=	1 bushel	=	———
16 ozs.	=	1 pound	=	———